THE POWER OF COMPUTATIONAL THINKING

Games, magic and puzzles to help you
become a computational thinker

THE POWER OF COMPUTATIONAL THINKING

Games, magic and puzzles to help you become a computational thinker

Paul Curzon
Peter W McOwan
Queen Mary University of London, UK

World Scientific

NEW JERSEY · LONDON · SINGAPORE · BEIJING · SHANGHAI · HONG KONG · TAIPEI · CHENNAI · TOKYO

Published by

World Scientific Publishing Europe Ltd.

57 Shelton Street, Covent Garden, London WC2H 9HE

Head office: 5 Toh Tuck Link, Singapore 596224

USA office: 27 Warren Street, Suite 401-402, Hackensack, NJ 07601

Library of Congress Cataloging-in-Publication Data

Names: Curzon, Paul. | McOwan, Peter W.

Title: The power of computational thinking : games, magic and puzzles to help you become a
    computational thinker / Paul Curzon (Queen Mary University of London, UK),
    Peter W. McOwan (Queen Mary University of London, UK).

Description: New Jersey : World Scientific, 2016.

Identifiers: LCCN 2016035729| ISBN 9781786341839 (hc : alk. paper) |
    ISBN 9781786341846 (pbk : alk. paper)

Subjects: LCSH: Computational learning theory. | Educational games. | Cognitive science.

Classification: LCC Q325.7 .C87 2016 | DDC 793.74--dc23

LC record available at https://lccn.loc.gov/2016035729

British Library Cataloguing-in-Publication Data

A catalogue record for this book is available from the British Library.

Desk Editors: Suraj Kumar/Mary Simpson

Typeset by Stallion Press
Email: enquiries@stallionpress.com

Printed in Singapore

Preface

Within just a few decades, computational thinking has changed the way we all live, work and play. It has changed the way science is done too; it has won wars; created whole new industries and saved lives. As the way computer scientists solve problems, computational thinking is at the heart of computer programming and is a powerful method of problem solving, with or without computers. It is so important that many countries now require that primary school children upwards learn the skills.

In 'The Power of Computational Thinking', we explain computational thinking in an accessible way using magic tricks, games and puzzles, as well as through real and challenging problems that computer scientists work on. We cover the elements of this form of problem solving, including algorithmic thinking, decomposition, abstraction, generalisation, logical thinking and pattern matching, whilst arguing that understanding people is vitally important for successful computational thinking. We also explore the links between computational thinking and scientific thinking, creativity and innovation.

Whether you simply want to know what computational thinking is all about, are looking for new ways to be effective, are starting out in computer science, or enjoy mathematical games and puzzles, then we wrote this book for you. It will give you a head start in learning the skills needed for both coding and designing new technologies more generally, as well as improving your real life problem solving skills.

It will help you understand both your own brain and the digital world in a deeper way, even showing you how to build a digital brain.

We hope that 'The Power of Computational Thinking' will show you that learning to think the computer scientist's way is fascinating fun.

About the Authors

Paul Curzon is a Professor of Computer Science at Queen Mary University of London. His research interests are computer science education, human computer interaction and formal methods. He was awarded a Higher Education Academy National Teaching Fellowship in 2010 and won the EPSRC Non-professional Computer Science Writer of the Year in 2007 in addition to several teaching prizes. He cofounded Teaching London Computing (www.teachinglondoncomputing.org), providing CPD support for teachers. Paul first taught himself to program on a beach in the South of France.

Peter McOwan is also a Professor of Computer Science at Queen Mary University of London. His research interests are in computer vision, artificial intelligence and robotics. He was awarded a Higher Education Academy National Teaching Fellowship in 2008 and the IET Mountbatten medal in 2011 for his work in promoting computer science to diverse audiences. Peter is an amateur magician with a healthy interest in science fiction.

Paul and Peter co-created the internationally known Computer Science for fun project (www.cs4fn.org) and were original members of the UK Computing at School network (CAS). Paul is now a board member of CAS.

Acknowledgements

This book is a compendium combining new material with reworked articles first written for our 'Computer Science for Fun' website and magazines (www.cs4fn.org), and our website to support computing and ICT teachers, 'Teaching London Computing' (www.teachinglondoncomputing.org).

We are grateful to Queen Mary University of London who have always given strong support for our public engagement work. Our work developing fun computer science material has been supported financially by many different organisations over the years including Queen Mary University of London, EPSRC, Google, the Mayor of London, the Department for Education, the BCS, RCUK, Microsoft and ARM.

Teachers across the country and beyond have been very encouraging. The teachers, academics, industry representatives, and others who form the UK Computing at School group, in particular, have been enormously supportive of our work and been very valuable for bouncing ideas and for trying out many of the activities. We are also grateful to the very many students and teachers over the last 10 years who we have inflicted our fun activities on for their enthusiasm, willingness to get involved and also for helping spark new ideas. Simon Peyton-Jones of Microsoft Research, Peter Dickman of Google and Bill Mitchell of the British Computer Society have been incredibly supportive. We have also been inspired by Tim Bell and Quintin Cutts and the teams involved in developing unplugged activities at the Universities of Canterbury and Glasgow, amongst many others. The Knights Tour activities, in particular, were inspired by and adapted from an idea by Maciej M. Sysło and Anna Beata Kwiatkowska of Nicolaus Copernicus University.

We have also been helped in numerous ways by members of staff at Queen Mary University of London, including Ursula Martin, Edmund Robinson and Sue White who helped us get cs4fn started. Gabriella Kazai and Jonathan Black did a lot of the hard work in the early days, and William Marsh, Jo Brodie, Nicola Plant, Jane Waite and Trevor Bragg more recently. Countless others have also helped.

As teenagers, we were especially inspired by Martin Gardner's recreational mathematics books, though it was only later we discovered most of the really interesting stuff was really computer science disguised as maths. We hope this book will similarly inspire some people helping them see straightaway that all the fun stuff is really computing. Don't be fooled when they call it maths!

We have had lots of useful discussions about maths and magic with Matt Parker, Jason Davison and Richard Garriott. We would also like to thank the ingenious magicians, past and present, who devised the clever mathematical tricks that use the computational algorithms we can now play with and teach. In particular, some of the notable magicians who have inspired us are Alex Elmsley, Karl Fulves, Nick Trost, J.,K. Hartman, Paul Gordon, Brent Morris, Colm Mulcahy, Arthur Benjamin, Max Maven, Aldo Colombini, Persi Diaconus, John Bannon and of course, again, the late great Martin Gardner. We recommend you track down their work and explore more about self-working magic. You will discover some amazing techniques, algorithms and ways to entertain, and perhaps uncover the greatest secret of them all, that magic (not to mention computational thinking) is a great hobby.

We would never have got into the game we are now in without many inspirational teachers who excited us about subjects not only Maths and science but just as importantly our English teachers who helped give us a love and understanding of writing.

Thanks most of all to our families for their enormous support and patience.

Contents

Chapter 1

Future Thinking

Computational thinking is an important skill set that computer scientists learn and use to solve problems. It's so important that in many countries all school kids are now expected to learn the skills. What is it, though? How has it changed the way we do just about everything? And why is it the basis of so much fun?

What Do You Do?

You are a scientist trying to understand the behaviour of birds feeding on the ground. Some feed, while others watch the sky for predators. How do they each decide which to do? Other scientists spend their time watching the birds, but you do more. You think about the algorithm — the sequence of steps — that the birds must be following as they decide what to do. You create a computer model and simulate different scenarios, based on your hypothesis that each bird watches its neighbours. It matches your observations of what birds do, but also makes predictions you can go out and test.

Maybe you are a magician. You've got an idea for a new trick based on a mathematical property of numbers. You develop the steps and the presentation, but will it always work? Rather than just trying it, you use logical reasoning and prove it always works. Except you find it doesn't. There is one situation where it could go wrong. A tweak of the presentation though and you make sure that situation will never happen.

You are a school student and the teacher is explaining how the brain works. They've drawn a picture of a neuron on the board, and labelled the parts that you are expected to learn. Overnight you write a program that behaves like a neuron. Linking several together, you start to see how a bunch of neurons really can do stuff. You use your program to explain it to your friends the next day.

Or perhaps you are a doctor frustrated at the way your medical staff make mistakes using some of the medical devices. The management blame the staff: one nurse was just sacked for making a mistake. You realise the problem is with the design of the device. It makes it easy for busy staff to miss a step. You talk to the manufacturers about how a slight change to the design will mean the problem never occurs again.

Perhaps you are a teacher with a giant pile of exam scripts that are in a random order. You need to sort them so that at the parents evening you can find any you want to talk about quickly. That's ok though. You know a really quick way to get them into order.

Maybe you get a holiday job in a coffee shop. You notice there are always long queues and the customers get frustrated. You point out to your Boss that part of the problem is that the person at the till spends a lot of time doing nothing. With a slight change to the way, the team works together it could all be faster.

Perhaps you are full of ideas for games that you know you and your friends would love to play. Unlike others, you don't just talk about your brilliant ideas, you write programs and within a few days you are playing them.

Computer Science is not just about computers, it is about computation that happens all over the place. Think like a computer scientist and you see computation and opportunities for improvement, opportunities for turning ideas into reality everywhere.

The 21st Century Skill Set

A bonus of learning Computer Science is that you learn a new and fundamental way of thinking, of solving problems; a way of thinking that is critical in the modern, technology-filled world. Called **Computational Thinking**, it is one of the big bonuses of studying computer science, whatever your ultimate career, and this idea is causing a big stir. In many countries, it is now considered so important that it has been added to reading, writing and arithmetic as a core ability that everyone should start to learn even at primary school. It is a way of thinking that has led to computers taking over large parts of our lives and changing everything we do from listening to music to trading stocks and shares, from the way we shop to the way we do science. It gives you the ability not just to have brilliant ideas but to turn them into reality.

The phrase 'Computational Thinking' was first used by the educationalist and mathematician, Seymour Papert. He was arguing for mathematics to be taught in a completely new way based on computation, but it's not just maths that has changed because of computer science, all science has. Computer Scientist, Jeannette Wing, argued that it is the most important part of learning computer science and is much more widely useful, and it was Jeanette who popularised the phrase. Microsoft, were sufficiently impressed by her arguments and the importance of the subject that they gave her university, Carnegie Mellon, a grant of several million dollars just to set up a centre to study this aspect of Computer Science and the way it transforms other sciences.

So what is Computational Thinking? It is not the way computers 'think', though increasingly we are programming them to use computational thinking too. It is a collection of diverse human skills to do with problem solving that result from studying the nature of computation. It draws on some obviously important skills that· most subjects help develop, like creativity, the ability to explain things clearly and team work. It pulls in ways of thinking from other subjects: thinking mathematically and scientifically, for example. At its core though are some very specific problem solving skills, such as the ability to think logically and algorithmically, with a focus on every last detail, as well as being able to devise efficient ways to do things. It is also about understanding people. Computer Science is unique in the way it brings all these diverse skills together. Together, they give a powerful way of thinking that is changing the world. That is how we have changed the way we do science, shop, run businesses, listen to music, play games, just about every aspect of our lives.

Algorithmic Thinking

Algorithmic thinking is at the core of computational thinking. It involves thinking of solutions to problems in a different way. To a computer scientist, the solution to a problem is not just an answer like '42'. Nor is it the achievement of something, like 'I just finished today's sudoku'. Solutions are algorithms! An *algorithm* is just a set of instructions to follow. If you follow the instructions in the algorithm exactly, you should get an actual answer to the problem (like 42) or achieve whatever you were trying to achieve (like complete the sudoku). Once you have an algorithmic solution you can get the answer to that problem without thinking at all: just follow the instructions 'blindly'. Once you have an algorithm that solves a problem, anyone can solve it without thinking. They don't even have to know or understand what the algorithm ultimately does. They might have no idea at all that they are solving a sudoku, for example (or even what one is). That also means a dumb machine, a computer, can also just mechanically follow the instructions and solve any instance of the problem too. That is all computers do, follow algorithms written by people.

The real power behind this idea is that following the algorithm gives solutions for a whole group of problems not just a single instance. An algorithm for solving crosswords would be able to solve lots of crosswords. An algorithm for doing arithmetic should be able to do any calculation. Thinking in this way about problems and solutions is called **algorithmic thinking**.

For example, knowing that 20 + 22 is 42 isn't good enough. A computer scientist wants an algorithm that can add any two numbers. In fact, everyone learns an algorithm to do this in primary school, precisely so they can do maths without having to work it all out for themselves! Similarly, all computers have the instructions of how to do addition built in, it is so important. Computers can only act as a calculator by following their instructions telling them how to do calculations. A computer program is just an algorithm or set of algorithms written in a language a computer can follow: a *programming language*.

Change the World

It isn't just calculations though. Algorithms can be used to do all sorts of things. Think algorithmically and you have a powerful way to change the world. If you write out an algorithm in the form of a program, then you can get them to blindly do all sorts of things. Banks now use algorithms instead of humans to do trading: to buy and sell so as to make millions of pounds of profit. NASA uses them to fly spaceships to Mars. You use algorithms to play music and videos. Algorithms fly aeroplanes, help surgeons and allow us to shop from our living room or while on a train. They drive cars. They are even creating art and music. Algorithms are now involved in all aspects of our lives. Algorithms have already transformed the way we live, and are continuing to do so. That is why understanding algorithmic thinking is so important for everyone. Just as we learn physics to understand the physical world and biology to understand the living world, we all need to learn some computer science to understand the virtual world that has silently taken over our lives.

Scientific Thinking

Algorithmic thinking is more than just a way to solve problems though. It gives a new way of understanding the world. The traditional sciences use experiments. Biologists do experiments on rats and monkeys, on cell cultures. Medics run drug trials. Physicists run experiments on the world itself. Think algorithmically though and there is an alternative. If we have a theory of how something works, whether it is the effect of radiation on the surface of a planet, how an ecosystem works or how cancer attacks cells, then we can create algorithms that work the same way. We can create a **computational model**: a program aiming to simulate the phenomena of interest. We can then do our experiments on the model too, rather than just on the real world. If our understanding is correct, then the program will behave like the thing it is intended to model. If it doesn't, then there is something wrong with our theory. By thinking about what has gone wrong, we can find ways to modify the theory and so improve our understanding. The model can also give us new predictions to go and test in the real world.

Computational Thinking

Computational thinking is more than just thinking of solutions as algorithms. It is a whole set of techniques that gives a powerful way to both improve things and to think about the world. Rather than work through lots of jargon though, we will introduce the ideas using example problems, both serious (like helping people with disabilities) and fun (using games, puzzles and magic).

Chapter 2

Searching to Speak

One of the worst medical conditions imaginable is locked-in syndrome. It leaves you totally paralysed except perhaps for the blink of an eye. Your intelligent mind is locked inside a useless body, able to sense everything but unable to communicate. It could happen to anyone, out of the blue, as a result of a stroke. If you wanted to help people with locked-in syndrome, the obvious thing might be to become a doctor or nurse, but how might a computer scientist help?

Locked-in Syndrome

Locked-in syndrome involves being totally paralysed as a result of having a stroke. You can still think, see, hear. You are as intelligent as you ever were. It could happen to anyone. There is no cure, so there isn't a lot medics can do beyond making their patients more comfortable. One big problem to tackle though is how to help people with locked-in syndrome 'talk'. How do they communicate with their doctors, family and friends. What a computer scientist might do then is obvious — they could invent some new technology to help. However, with some computational thinking, we can give a much better answer than just "we need technology".

'The Diving Bell and the Butterfly' is an incredibly uplifting book. It's the autobiography of *Jean-Dominique Bauby*, written after he woke up in a hospital bed, totally paralysed. In the book, he describes life with locked-in syndrome. He did have a way to communicate, not only with medics, friends and family, but also to write the book. He did it without any technology at all. How?

Put yourself in his position, waking up in a hospital bed. How could you communicate? How could you write a book? You have only a person facing you with a pen and paper ready to write down your 'words'. You are one of the lucky ones, you can blink one eye, but that is all you can do. You can't move in any other way. That means you can't speak. You can see and hear though.

Now imagine you are his doctor. You must come up with a way for him to communicate.

Simple as A, B, C

What you need is to agree a way of turning blinks (that's all he can do) into letters. Your first idea might be to tell him that one blink means 'A', two blinks means 'B' and so on. The helper then just has to count the blinks and write down the corresponding letter.

In coming up with this idea, we are already thinking like a computer scientist. What we are doing is the core of computational thinking: **algorithmic thinking**. We have come up with a series of steps that we and the helper can follow that will guarantee the letters the patient is thinking of are communicated. A computer scientist calls this agreed way of communicating an *algorithm*: a series of steps to follow in a given order that achieves some goal (here to communicate letters and words). **Algorithmic thinking** is about coming up with algorithms to solve problems.

The beauty of algorithms is that the steps can be followed without those involved having any understanding of what they are doing. With our algorithm, the helper presumably would know what they were doing and why, but the book would still get written even if they didn't. All the helper needs to do is count blinks and write down the letters according to the instructions they have been given. We could even give them a table to look up the letters in so they could do it without any thought at all. The beauty of algorithms is that they allow people to do things 'mechanically' like this — and that's the key as it means computers can blindly follow the instructions too. That is, all computers can do: blindly follow their instructions.

Our algorithm for communicating actually comes in two parts. There is one part for Bauby to follow (blink the right number of times) and one for the helper (count the number of blinks and write down the corresponding letter when the blinks stop). In fact, computer scientists have a special name for this kind of algorithm that passes information between 2 people or computers — it's called a *protocol*. If both people follow their part of the protocol, then the words Bauby is thinking will end up written on the piece of paper. If either makes a mistake — losing count, for example, so not following the protocol — then the message won't get through. The great thing about computers is they don't get things wrong like that: they follow their instructions exactly, every time. As long as the instructions are right, they will always do it right.

Algorithmic thinking is a particular kind of problem solving — one where you don't just come up with a single answer, like the one thing that Bauby wanted to say when he first woke up. You come up with a solution in terms of steps that others (including a computer) can follow to get answers. We just came up with a solution like that for Bauby. It doesn't just tell us what he is trying to say now. It is a way we (and anyone else in future) can always work out what he wants to say. It sounds pretty slow though. Maybe there is a better way. Thinking about better, more efficient, solutions is also a part of **algorithmic thinking**.

How did Bauby do it?

Bauby did have a better way, a better algorithm, and he describes it in his book. Remember that the helper can speak, so we can make use of that. The algorithm Bauby used involved the helper reading the alphabet aloud "A ... B... C...". When the letter he was thinking of was spoken, he blinked. The helper wrote that letter down and then started again, letter after letter. Try it with a friend. Communicate your initials to them that way. Then think about that being the only way you have to talk to anyone. I hope your name isn't Zebedee Zacharius Zog or Zara Zootle!

Now think about life like that. Talking to friends and family has to be done like that. So does talking to doctors and nurses. If you want someone to open the curtains or change the TV channel, then that is how you have to ask for it to be done.

Once you've tried it, you may have realised there are some more problems we have to solve to really make it work. Having tried it a few times, you might also be able to think of other ways to improve the algorithm. What can you come up with?

Checking the Details

One thing you may have worked out is that there is more than the 26 letters to deal with. We need spaces, digits, full stops, commas and so on, too. We need to add them to the list of letters the helper works through. Perhaps there is a better way than one long list. Perhaps the first question could be: "Is it a letter?" If it is, we carry on as before. If not, we start working through the other symbols. Does that sound familiar? It is the idea word processors use of having separate character sets.

Another thing to deal with is what happens if the person blinks by mistake? We need a way to say; "Ignore that last blink and start the letters again". You don't want to have to spell that out letter by letter! Similarly if we just made a mistake, we need a way to back up. We need a code that means "undo". Having a way to undo things is an important part of any algorithm that involves people as people make mistakes. One way for our problem might be to agree that blinking twice quickly means that. Maybe you can think of a better way. Perhaps you thought of other problems that need solving too?

Checking an algorithm works both in theory and practice in this way is an important part of computational thinking: **evaluation**. Whenever we come up with a new algorithm, we need to check it works very carefully. Programmers spend more time evaluating their programs (which remember are just algorithms for a computer to follow) than actually writing them in the first place. It is all too easy to get a detail wrong, or forget some situation that might occasionally arise and so that the algorithm has to deal with. The point of an algorithm is that it works every time, whatever happens.

Algorithmic thinking is thinking about all the details and finding solutions to problems that arise. It's about realising there can be many ways of doing things, and then coming up with the best one for this particular situation. Notice too that one of the problems we thought of above was about what people do: making mistakes. In theory, our solution works: just blink at the right time! We could arrogantly say the people should just do the right thing and it's their fault if they get it wrong. In practice, they will sometimes blink at the wrong time. It's better if we solve the problem in a way that does work for people. After all, it is the person we are trying to help, not a machine! Computational thinking is about understanding people too.

Doing it Better

What's next?

We can speed things up for our locked-in patient if we realise that sometimes halfway through a word we can guess what it is. If you have got "a-n-t-e-l" it would be a pretty good bet to assume the word was antelope. So we can change the rules to allow the helper to make guesses like that. We need a way for the person to say no after a guess though. Perhaps the rule could be that they just blink if the word is right, and do nothing if not. This is of course how *predictive texting* on your phone works. It's the algorithm phones use, faced with a very similar problem. Search engines do the same thing as you type in a word to search for.

Bauby's helpers did use a version of predictive texting and he describes it in the book. He also describes how infuriating it could be when people did it without agreeing the algorithm for him to say yes or no first. Their lack of computational thinking led to him having a frustrating time trying to tell them they were wrong, when they were sure they had guessed a word. For example, if we were still talking about animals and I spelled out h-o-r ... what would you guess? Horse perhaps? No. I was spelling out Hornbill.

Perhaps you thought of the idea of guessing whole words too, and maybe you got the idea because you had used predictive texting! If you did, then you've just used another computational thinking skill: **pattern matching**. Often problems turn out to be essentially the same as something you've already seen in a different situation. If you already have a solution for that other problem, then you can just reuse it. **Pattern matching** is the skill of spotting that a new situation is essentially the same as something you've come across before and realising that an old solution can be reused.

Algorithms are a way of giving this kind of general solution. We can reuse the predictive texting solution because a phone and the helper both have the same problem. The phone must work out what words are being typed letter by letter and the helper must work out the word someone with locked-in syndrome is thinking letter by letter. Once we realise that similarity, then any solution we come up with for one can be used for the other. Better still we might realise that we have a solution that works for lots of different problems and create a description of the algorithm at the outset that we will be able to reuse whenever the situation arises. That is called **generalisation** of the algorithm. **Generalisation** is a very powerful computational thinking trick. Very generally, we can think of what we are doing here as communicating information. In any situation where we need to communicate, we can use the general algorithm. Computer Scientists build up collections of algorithms for different kinds of problems, so that whenever they come across a version of that problem, they can just choose the best one for the situation. For example, another algorithm for communicating information is *Morse code*: using different sequences of dots and dashes (think short and long blink) as a code for the different letters. It was invented to send messages by telegraph, but perhaps it could be used here too. We will return to that idea.

Even more generally, we can think of what we are doing as searching for a piece of information (the next letter). We can perhaps generalise our algorithm to allow us to search for anything. We will return to that idea later too.

How Common

Bauby actually realised that the ABC algorithm could be improved upon in a different way. He had been the Editor-in-chief of the French women's magazine, Elle, before that hospital bed, so knew a lot about language. He knew that some letters are more common than others in human languages. E is the most common letter (in both English and French), for example. He therefore got the helper to read out the letters in order of how common they are: their *frequency*. In English, the order is "E...T...A...O...". In French, Bauby's language, it is "E...S...A...R..." Being French, he spoke French so he used the French order. That way the helper got to the common letters more quickly.

A similar trick has been used through the ages to crack secret codes and is called *frequency analysis*. The algorithm of using letter frequencies was actually invented by Muslim scholars over a 1000 years ago. In fact, Mary Queen of Scots was beheaded because Queen Elizabeth I's spymaster Sir Francis Walsingham was better at computational thinking in this way than she was. That's another story though. Bauby's idea of using frequency analysis is an example of both **pattern matching** and **generalisation**: of transforming problems and reusing solutions. Once we have recognised that cracking codes and guessing letters are similar problems, we can see that the frequency analysis solution invented for one can be used for the other.

How Fast is That?

Let's get back to Bauby's algorithm. We've improved things for sure. The new way must be better than our original idea of blinking different times for each letter. An obvious question though is how fast actually is it: "How long did it take to write that book?" Is it the best we can possibly do, or could we come up with a faster algorithm, and so have helped him write the book much more easily?

We need a way of measuring how good an algorithm is. One way would be to do it experimentally: using **scientific thinking**. For each algorithm we think up, we could time how long it takes to communicate some specific passage. We could do this lots of times with lots of people and see which way is fastest on average. That would take a vast amount of time and effort, though. There is a better way.

We can do some **analytical thinking**. We will use some simple maths to work out an answer. First, rather than think about time let's think about the work done. If we count how many letters of the alphabet the helper has to say, then we can always turn that into the time taken later. We would just need to know how long it takes to say one letter and multiply that time by the number of letters. We have just done something called **abstraction**. It's another part of computational thinking, used to simplify problems and make programs easier to write. **Abstraction** is just a long word meaning to hide or ignore some of the details. We have ignored the detail of precise times and instead counted letters spoken. We are using "number of letters said" as an **abstraction** of the actual time taken. The idea is used throughout computing as a way of making things easier to do.

So how do we work out how many letters have to be said? There are several questions we can ask. The simplest is: what is the *best case*? What is the fewest number of letters the helper could possibly have to say to write the book? We could also look at the *worst case*. If we are unlucky, how bad could it be? Finally, we can look at the *average case*: that will give us a realistic estimate of how much work it actually took. Let's, for the sake of argument, stick to communicating just letters of the alphabet without digits and punctuation. We will analyse our simple algorithm of the helper saying A, B, C, . . .

In the best case, the whole book would be nothing but A's: "AAAA . . ." (perhaps expressing the pain he is in). To communicate a single letter 'A', we just say one letter 'A' (one question) and we have the answer. We are using **abstraction** here again, analysing counting a single letter initially, ignoring the whole book, at least to start with. Multiply our answer for one letter by the number of letters in the book and we have the best case for writing the whole book.

The worst case, perhaps telling a story where someone snores the whole time, "ZZZZ . . .", takes 26 questions to get each letter. We have worked out the bounds on what communicating anything would be. It's always no better than one and no worse than 26 letters spoken per letter communicated.

A closer estimate would be the average number of questions asked per letter: the average case. But that's easy to work out. In a long message, for every 'A', roughly on average there will also be a 'Z' somewhere else in the message. For every 'B' there will be a 'Y', and so on. That means on average over the whole book 13 questions will be asked per letter dictated. Multiply the number of letters in the book by 13 and you have an estimate for how much work was done to write it. Multiply that by the average time for the helper to say a letter and you have the time needed to write the book.

Notice we are evaluating our algorithm again here, but rather than asking whether it works as we were before, this time we are asking how quickly it works. There are lots of different aspects of an algorithm we can evaluate, but whether it always works and whether it works efficiently are two of the most important aspects of **evaluation**.

Bauby's modification, asking about common letters first, improves things: maybe it will be down to 10 or 11 letters spoken. You can work that out more precisely using the frequencies of the letters. Either look up the frequencies, or perhaps work it out yourself. Take a section of your favourite book and count the number of times each letter appears. Put the letters in order of most common with the probability for each. Then add up the probabilities. The average case is the number of letters needed for the probability of those letters to add up to 50.

So frequency analysis is an improvement, but its not a lot better and the worst case for a letter is still 26. As any computer scientist knows, though, we can do far better. It is possible to work out each letter with only five questions! Guaranteed! That's not the average case, it's the worst case! Can you work out what five questions you need to ask?

20 Questions?

Do it in 5

Whether you came up with the answer or not, I guarantee you know what the right sort of question is, but only if we look at a different problem.

Let's play a game of 20 questions: the children's game where I think of a famous person and you try and guess who I'm thinking of by asking me questions. The twist is that I will only ever answer yes or no. Play a game with a friend, thinking about the kind of questions you ask as you do. Let's see how a game might go.

"Are you female?" No
"Are you alive?" No
"Were you a film star?" No
"Were you from Britain?" Yes
"Were you a writer?" Yes
"Were you alive in the 20th century?" No
"Were you alive in the 19th century?" No
"Are you Shakespeare?" Yes

Chances are when you played the game, you asked similar questions. You almost certainly didn't start by asking questions like "Is it Aristotle?", "Is it James Bond?", "Is it Marie Curie?" You would never get the answer in 20 questions that way. You only ask that sort of question at the end when you are pretty sure you know who it is (as we just did). Instead you probably asked a question like "Are you female?" first.

Why is that a good first question? Well, it's because it rules out half the possibilities, whatever the answer. If you ask "Is it the Queen?" then you rule out millions if you are right, but if wrong (more likely) you only rule out one person. You would have to be lottery-winning lucky to do well that way. So the secret to playing 20 questions is to ask questions that rule out half the people each time, whatever the answer.

How Good is That?

Asking halving questions is better than naming people one at a time, but how much better? Let's suppose I might be thinking of one of a million people at the start. If I rule out half the people with each question, how many questions does it take? After one question, we are down to 500,000 people left, after two questions 250,000,... After 10 questions, there are only about 1000 people left out of the original million it could be (see Figure 1). Keep going...500 left after another question, 250, 125, ... and on the 20th question there is only possible person left. If you can ask perfect halving questions

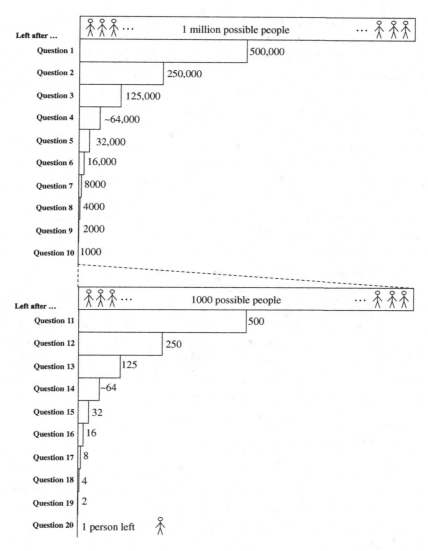

Figure 1: Repeated halving from a million to 1 takes only 20 questions.

every time you are guaranteed to win. You will *always* do it in 20 questions.

This is all **algorithmic thinking**, of course. We have been trying to work out an algorithm for playing 20 questions. We haven't come up with a full algorithm though, we haven't actually worked out a way of coming up with the questions. That is your problem when playing the game. We are using another computational thinking trick: **decomposition**. We are splitting the problem (decomposing it) into different parts so that we can focus on each separately. We've come up with the overall strategy. It's a separate problem to come up with the individual halving questions.

Decomposition is a common problem solving strategy, but it turns out to be a vital tool for computer scientists. The problems they have to solve writing programs or designing processors (like the ones in your laptop or phone) are massive. Modern computer chips are more complicated than the road network of the whole of the planet Earth. Imagine trying to design that in one go. It is only possible by decomposing it into parts you can work on separately.

Decomposition relies on **abstraction**, hiding detail. Here, we are hiding the detail of the exact questions asked; only thinking about the kind of question. We were also using **decomposition** when thinking about how efficient our original algorithm was. We decomposed the problem of determining the work needed to write a book into the problem of determining the work needed to communicate individual letters, and the problem of converting that into the work needed for the whole book.

A New Algorithm

So, with the right questions, in the worst case, it takes only 20 questions to find the person I am thinking of out of a million possibilities. Compare that with our previously saying it takes 13 questions (and worst case 26) to find one thing out of 26 letters of the alphabet. Yes/No is no different to Blink/No-blink. When we asked, is it A? Is it B? we were doing the equivalent of asking "Are you Mickey Mouse?", "Are you Nelson Mandela?" You are trying to work out one of many things I am thinking of, just the same. It is actually the same problem again, just like predictive texting was!

If it's the same problem as working out a letter a person is thinking, then surely the same strategy will give us a better solution than the ones we came up with so far. We are using **pattern matching** and **generalisation** here again. We are transforming problems to reuse the solutions. What is the equivalent of our halving solution for letters of the alphabet? We could ask "Is it a vowel?" first perhaps, but what then for the other four questions? We need to halve the alphabet each time. The obvious first question then is "Is it between A and M?" If the answer was "yes", then we next ask, "Is it between A and F?" If the answer was "no", we ask "Is it between N and S?" instead, and so on. That way we are sure to get to any letter of the alphabet that the person is thinking of in only five questions as shown in the *decision tree* of Figure 2. Start at the top of the diagram and follow the paths according to the yes/no answers given. You will always get to a letter in five questions at worst.

This is where another part of **algorithmic thinking** comes in. We need to be sure we agree on the detail as there is scope for confusion. When we say "Is it between A and M?" we need to be clear whether we are including M (we were).

We can even improve things more using the frequency analysis trick. With only 26 letters we could, for example, make it so we get the letter E and a few other common letters faster than five questions. Try and come up with a version of the decision tree that does that. We could also still use the predictive texting trick to

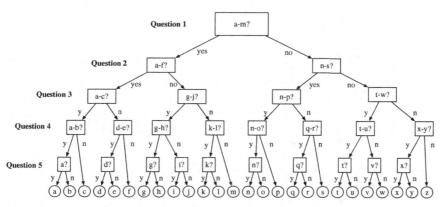

Figure 2: A decision tree showing questions to ask to get to any letter of the alphabet in five questions or less.

guess words that were only partly completed, too. All those solutions from our earlier algorithm still apply here. We are again reusing past solutions.

Codes for Letters

The decision tree might suggest a rather different solution. If we think of the Yes and No or blink and no-blink as 1 and 0, then the decision tree defines a binary sequence that the person with locked-in syndrome has to communicate for each letter (see Figure 3).

To speed things up, we could therefore drop the need for questions. The person communicating just needs to go through the sequence for each letter, and the other person takes note. So for example, blinking the code 0110 (no-blink, blink, blink, no-blink) would communicate the letter p. We could therefore turn the decision tree into a *lookup table* like Figure 4. We could just give either the decision tree or the table to anyone wishing to communicate so they can decipher the blinks. We have essentially just invented a Morse code-like code for communicating. Again we see that the problem we have been thinking about is essentially the same as the one Samuel

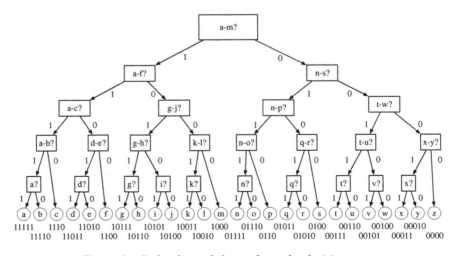

Figure 3: Codes for each letter from the decision tree.

Code	Letter	Code	Letter
11111	a	01111	n
11110	b	01110	o
1110	c	0110	p
11011	d	01011	q
11010	e	01010	r
1100	f	0100	s
10111	g	00111	t
10110	h	00110	u
10101	i	00101	v
10100	j	00100	w
10011	k	00011	x
10010	l	00010	y
1000	m	00000	z

Figure 4: A lookup table giving the letters for each binary sequence.

Morse was trying to solve to allow communication by telegraph. Dots and dashes correspond to our 1s and 0s or blinks and no-blinks. **Generalisation** yet again.

However, we need to be careful about rushing to a solution. The detail matters. If there are no questions being asked, how does anyone know when the person is communicating and when not. If they don't blink are they saying "zzzzzzzzz" or are they not saying anything? How do we tell when the blinks for a letter starts. How long does a no-blink actually last? Our small change has introduced lots of new problems to solve. Samuel Morse did solve them. In fact, Morse code uses three symbols to solve these problems not two: dots, dashes and silence. The lengths of each are specified precisely. However long a dot is, the silence between dots and dashes is the same. The silence between letters is three times that, and between words seven times the length of a dot. This provides the structure we've lost by dropping the questions.

This code solution worked really well for the telegraph and a variation is the basis of how computers communicate over networks. Whether this is actually a better solution in our locked-in syndrome situation is a moot point though. Being precise with timings, while being easy for machines to follow, is all a lot harder than just asking questions in our human situation.

Choosing the Best Solution

Search algorithms

Our solutions for 20 questions carried over to helping a paralysed person speak because the problem was essentially the same. It is a *search problem*: given a series of things, find the particular one we are looking for. The solutions to this problem are called *search algorithms*. They are sure-fire ways of finding things. Our first approach of checking each of the possibilities in turn (Is it A?, Is it B?... Is it Adele? Is it Bond? ...) is an algorithm called *linear search*. Sometimes it's the best you can do. For example, if you see a robbery and the police set up an identity parade, you couldn't do better than linear search: check each face in turn until you see the person in the line that did it. Linear search works well when there is no order to the things you are searching through. If you are searching for a missing sock that could be in any drawer of your chest of drawers, then start at the top and check the drawers one at a time.

Our other algorithm involved finding halving questions: Is it before N? Are they female? Finding halving questions is a general problem solving strategy called *Divide and conquer*. If you can come up with a divide and conquer solution to a problem, it is likely to be very fast. Why? Because as we saw repeated halving gets you down to one answer very quickly, and far, far faster than checking one thing at a time. Notice we are doing **generalisation** again. The simplest divide and conquer search algorithm is called *binary search*. Imagine lining all the things you are searching through in order, smallest at one end, largest at the other. Binary search involves going to the middle item and checking whether the thing you are looking for comes before or after it. You then discard the other half and do the same again on what is left. You keep doing that until only one thing remains: the thing you were looking for. That is probably close to what you do if given a big paper telephone directory and you want to find a particular name. You certainly wouldn't start at the first page and check each name in turn until you find the one you are looking for!

There are many more search algorithms than just these two. For example, how does a search engine like Google search through every web page on the planet in fractions of a second? It needs a better algorithm still!

The idea of having a search algorithm involves **abstraction**. We abstract from the details of the particular problem and see it as just a search problem. Then our search algorithm is a ready-made solution for lots of problems. Thinking about it another way, once we have come up with a strategy to win at 20 questions, we can generalise that solution to the idea of divide and conquer: we have a general strategy that works for other problems too. **Abstraction** and **generalisation** often go hand in hand.

Improving Life for Bauby

So Bauby should have got the helper to ask halving questions. Think about it. Five questions at worst rather than 13 on average, multiplied up by all the letters in his book. It's not only the book either, it's talking with his friends and family, the doctors and nurses too. If only he had known some computer science, how much easier his life would have been!

Algorithmic Thinking First

The thing to notice is we haven't been looking at technology at all, so far. It has all been about two people 'talking'. Now we have worked out a good way, a good algorithm, we can think how we could automate it with suitable technology. We could build an *eye tracking* system that detects blinks or an *electrode cap* that can pick up whether Bauby is thinking yes or no, perhaps. The point is that whatever technology we use, it would need a search algorithm underneath it. Pick the wrong one and however good the technology is, the communication will still be slow: 13 questions instead of five. It makes no difference whether the helper is a computer or a human for that. If we hadn't thought about the algorithms first we could have come up with a frustratingly slow system. Computing is not just about the technology it is about the computational thinking needed to devise good solutions.

Understanding People First

So we all agree with a little bit more computational thinking Bauby's life could have been improved. But wait a minute. Perhaps we got it wrong. Perhaps we would have ensured his book was never completed and his life was even more a hell. Why? We did not start with technology but we did start with computer science. Perhaps we should have started with the person. Were we counting the right thing?

As our measure of work, our **abstraction**, we used the number of questions asked. Asking questions is the job of the helper and it may be tedious but it's not difficult. What if blinking was a great effort for Bauby. His solution involved him blinking only once per letter. Our divide and conquer algorithm requires him to blink five times. Multiply that by a whole book. We could have made it five times harder for him! It could be blinking is easy and our algorithm is better. We don't know the answer, because we didn't ask the question. We should have asked first. Bauby didn't say in the book, and it is probably different for each person. We should have started with the person.

Furthermore, his solution is easy for anyone to walk in and understand. Ours is more complex to follow and might need some explaining before the visitor understands. Bauby is not going to be the one to do the explaining. Thinking about people is important.

This highlights another vitally important aspect of **evaluation** of algorithms: evaluating whether our solutions work in practice for people. Are people able to use them easily without making mistakes and do they have a good experience in doing so? This applies even if a computer is following the algorithm itself, if people have to then interact with the program. This is called *usability* and *user experience*. This kind of **evaluation** ultimately has to involve trying out solutions with real people. The sooner we do it the better.

It Worked for Him

One thing is certain about Bauby's solution, it worked for him. He wrote a whole book that way after all. Perhaps the helper did more than just write down his words. Perhaps they opened the curtains, talked to him about the outside world or just provided some daily human warmth. Perhaps the whole point of writing the book was that it gave him an excuse to have a person there to communicate with all the time, paid for by his publisher!

The communication algorithm would not then be about the needs of the book, but about the book helping a deep need for direct communication with a person. Replace the human with technology and perhaps you have replaced the thing that was actually keeping him alive.

On the other hand, perhaps once he is able to talk to a computer, he can get out of his hospital bed into the virtual world, emailing friends, using social networking in all its forms, controlling an avatar, perhaps one day even controlling a robot version of himself that moves around the real world in his place... Perhaps we have made things better.

The point is we need to find out what he really wants and needs first. In an extreme usability situation like this, the important thing is that the user really is involved throughout. We call this *user-centred design*. One of the most powerful versions is called *participative design*: the ultimate users actually help come up with the design ideas rather than just being involved in evaluating them. That is essentially what Bauby did. He got directly involved in designing the way he communicated. In fact, user-centred design is a better way when designing *any system* for people, not just in extreme situations. It is they who ultimately have to adapt what's available to make it work for them, not only technically but also emotionally and socially. Otherwise, we may devise a 'solution' that is wonderful in theory but in practice hell on earth. Computer Scientists have to think about much more than just computers.

Chapter 3

Magic and Algorithms

The skills you need to be a great stage magician, inventing magic tricks, are the same as those you need to be a great computer scientist: computational thinking. Magic tricks are algorithms and that is all a computer program is too. When early computers searched for data, they were actually doing a magic trick called the Australian Magician's Dream. Computer programmers really are wizards!

The Australian Magician's Dream

The mechanics of predicting the future

In the magic trick, 'The Australian Magician's Dream', the magician predicts a revealed card that no one could possibly have known in advance. At its core is some important computer science. Here's how to do the trick.

Before starting, out of sight of the audience, take an ordinary shuffled pack of cards and place the Eight of Hearts in the 16th position from the top of the face down pack. Place a distinctive card (e.g., the Ace of Hearts) in the 32nd position. Place the pack face down on the table, so the Eight of Hearts should now be 16th from the top. Next take the Eight of Hearts from a second pack (ideally from an over-sized pack for extra effect) and place it in a sealed envelope. Put the envelope under the table where it will remain in full sight throughout the trick.

Now for the part the audience see. Get a volunteer to the front. Spread the cards in a line across the table, face up so they can see it is a normal shuffled pack. Announce that first you need to roughly halve the pack. Spread your hands, to show what you mean, asking them to point to a card of their choice roughly in the middle. Secretly make sure your hands are over the 16th and the 32nd card. This casually, but importantly, limits the volunteer's choice when dividing the pack to a point between those two positions. Discard all the cards to the right of the one they point to (the bottom of the pack), confirming with them that it was their free choice. Pick up the remaining cards and, holding them face down, explain that the night before you do magic shows you always have weird dreams where magicians teach you new tricks. You had a dream last night where an Australian magician came to you and taught you the "Down-Under Deal": a way to end up with a card that no one could possibly know in advance.

Now deal out the cards, alternately placing them into two piles. While doing this say, "Down" as you put cards face down in the first pile. Say "Under" as you put cards face up in the second pile. Once all the cards have been dealt, discard the 'Down' pile, noting you always throw away that pile. Pick up the 'under' pile, turning them face down, and repeat the process, discarding the 'down' pile every time. Continue to do this until you are left with one card on the table in the face up 'under' pile. It will be the Eight of Hearts. Tell the audience that this is the selected card. Have them confirm they had no idea of what the resulting card would be and get them to show it to the audience saying what card it is. Get the volunteer to confirm they had a free choice in where they split the pack. Turn the top few cards of the discard pile over to show "had you split the pack one card differently, it would have been a different card".

Now point out that the weird thing is that in your dream, the Australian magician told you to place one particular card in an envelope. Ask the volunteer to look "Down Under the table" and reveal the card in the envelope that was predicted by the Australian Magician in your dream. It is also the Eight of Hearts!

Thank the volunteer and ask the audience to give them a round of applause for helping.

Tricky Algorithms

What does a magic trick have to do with computing? Well, this kind of trick, which a magician would call a *self-working trick*, is exactly what a computer scientist calls an *algorithm*. It's a series of instructions that if followed in the given order always results in a specific, desired effect. In this case, the effect is the magical effect that the card you end up with is the one predicted. Computer programs are just algorithms written in a language that a computer, rather than a human magician, can follow. The effect is whatever the programmer wanted the program to do.

The algorithm behind the Australian Magician's dream is given in Figure 5.

The steps in this particular algorithm aren't just a simple sequence of steps to be followed one after the other. They include loops like: "Repeat 4 times". A loop is just a way of writing that some instructions are to be repeated. It lets you avoid having to write out the same thing lots of times. That is exactly the kind of instruction used by programmers in computer programs to tell a computer to repeat some instruction. There is also a second loop: "Repeat until no cards left". That loop is repeated four times by the first loop. Each of those four times you go through the pack until no cards are left, keeping then discarding cards.

To do the Australian Magician's Dream:
Place the chosen card in position 16.
Place the prediction in an envelope
Discard roughly the bottom half of the pack
Repeat 4 times:
    Repeat until no cards are left:
        Discard a card
        Keep a card
Open the envelope to reveal the card is the one predicted.

Figure 5: The algorithm for the Australian Magician's Dream.

Inventing Tricks

To invent a new magic trick, a magician has to do all the same kind of thinking that a computer scientist does: computational thinking. A card trick is computation, just computation done physically with a pack of cards instead of in a computer. The core of inventing any new magic trick is **algorithmic thinking**. The magician has to come up with a series of steps they can follow that will *always* lead to the magical effect happening. After all they don't want the trick *ever* to fail to work. They don't want to look silly on stage. That means they have to think about every last detail. They need to be sure of the order the steps need to be done in. Just as with programming, they have to think about every eventuality. Could the volunteer do something that would lead to it not working? If so, they have to know what to do. They also have to record the trick in a form that is precise enough that in future they, or someone else, will be able to follow the steps again and make the trick work (though Magicians tend to be secretive people rather than the sharing people that most computer scientists are!). This is all **algorithmic thinking** in action.

The main point though is that once a magician has invented a trick and written down the algorithm (in a book of runes perhaps!), anyone who then has the algorithm can do the trick. They don't have to do any of the clever invention part themselves. All they have to do is follow the instructions exactly. The Sorcerer's Apprentice can do the trick even if they have no idea how or why it works. Do the steps correctly and precisely and they will get the correct magical effect.

Why does this matter to computer scientists? That is exactly what you need to make a computer work. They are just lumps of metal and silicon. They understand nothing about what they do. All they do is follow the instructions blindly like a sorcerer's apprentice. Programmers do all the creative, inventive part in coming up with the instructions. Programming involves the skill of writing instructions in very clear and precise ways so that there is no way for things to be done in the wrong way. There can be no doubt about what is intended by each instruction: a computer has to follow them and it will follow them precisely. Every eventuality has to be covered by the instructions, as a computer can't deal with something unexpected. By following the instructions, though, computers can do amazing things (and even seem intelligent as we will see).

Every computer gadget you ever saw do anything was just blindly following an algorithm.

Split It Up

One way a magician might create a new trick is to build it out of its parts, working on the steps and presentation of each part separately. This is computational thinking in action again: **decomposition**. The Australian Magician's Dream trick combines four main parts. The first is to setup the pack by placing cards in known positions. The second is in discarding the bottom part of the pack, making the volunteer think they had a free choice that might have made a difference (when it doesn't). The next step is the dealing process to end up with a single card. The final step is the reveal to see the prediction. Writing the trick out as an algorithm at that level of detail gives us something like Figure 6(a).

Note how we are doing **abstraction** here: hiding detail. In this description, we have hidden the detail of how the steps are done. We don't say how to repeatedly discard every second card. We can

To do the Australian Magician's Dream:
    Set up the trick
    Discard roughly half of the pack
    Repeatedly discard every second card
    Reveal the card is the one predicted

(a) An abstract version of the algorithm for the Australian Magician's Dream.

To Repeatedly discard every second card:
    Repeat 4 times:
        Repeat until no cards left:
            Discard a card
            Keep a card

(b) The algorithm for discarding every second card.

Figure 6: Using decomposition to describe the Australian Magician's Dream.

write up those details as their own mini-algorithm. For example, an algorithm for the step of repeatedly discarding every second card is given in Figure 6(b).

In fact, we already did that kind of abstraction for each of the other steps in the original version of the algorithm. Why? Because we wanted you to get the overall idea without being bogged down in the detail.

This kind of **decomposition** makes it much easier to understand an algorithm. We only need to look at the details if, and when, we need to understand how they are done, not what they do. If you want a crib sheet to help you remember the steps (may be written on the back of your hand), you might write the simpler abstracted version. You can't write every detail as you'd never be able to read it. Or perhaps you would just write the detail of a single step that you know you keep forgetting. **Decomposition** can help you get it right.

Having decomposed our trick into its separate parts, we could use the components in other tricks too. For example, lots of tricks involve revealing a prediction. One way that can be done is by putting a prediction in an envelope in full sight of everyone as we have done. There are other ways though. You could video a friend holding up the predicted card instead and play the video, for example. That is one of the beauties of decomposition. We don't have to reuse whole solutions, we can reuse (and **generalise**) parts of solutions. Any time a trick needs a 'reveal' we can pull out this solution.

Decomposition also allows us to swap in new versions of parts of a trick to improve it, replacing them with alternative ways to do the same thing. For example, suppose we have this great new idea for the Australian Magician's Dream of putting the prediction inside a balloon that we have as a decoration on stage. It is just another way of doing Step 4, but this time with a bang! We can work out the details in a balloon version of the reveal algorithm, and swap them into our instructions without changing the top level algorithm. Of course, there are two steps that then need to change: the set up and the reveal. We can't change one without the other. However, the other parts of the trick don't have to change at all. Programmers write programs in the same way as lots of self-contained parts.

Does the Trick Always Work?

This trick works because if you repeatedly discard every second card, you are guaranteed to end up with the 16th card. Is it really guaranteed? Do you trust me enough, when I say that, that you are now willing to do the trick live on stage, just because I've told you it always works? Or would you like some evidence? Science is all about not just trusting claims people make but demanding hard evidence! We need to evaluate the algorithm so we can be sure it really does work every time.

How can we be sure though? One way is to try it over and over again. If it works every time, we do it that gives us some confidence it really does always work. Programmers call this *testing*. The more tests you do, the more confidence you have. But how can we be sure that the next time, the time we do it for an audience, won't be the one time it doesn't work? Could we test every possibility? Well that would mean trying it with every possible order a pack of cards could be in when we start the trick. For each of those orders, we would have to check it worked for all the places the pack might be split by the volunteer. That is far too many possibilities to check than is practical.

If we use a bit of **logical thinking** instead, we don't have to do all those tests though.The first thing to notice is that the values of the cards other than the 16th card don't matter at all. They could all be blank and it would not change the logic of what happens in the trick. It would be less magical of course, but thats not the point here. We are never going to do the trick that way, it is just to help us think. It means we can just reason about the cards based on their position rather than their value. We are doing **abstraction** (again): hiding some of the detail of the problem (the values of the cards this time) to make it easier to reason about.

That narrows down the testing we have to do. We just need to check it works wherever we split the pack. Will we always end up with the 16th card whatever card the volunteer points to? There are only 52 positions we could split the pack, so we now know we could get away with only testing those 52 cases and checking in every case the 16th card is the one left. Probably by now you can see that actually it won't always work! We need a way to restrict where we do the split...

Programmers face a similar problem testing programs. They can't test all the things people could possibly do using their program. They therefore use **logical thinking** to build a *test plan*: a set of tests that if passed will give a strong (if not always perfect) assurance that the program works as it should.

Fifty-two times is still a lot of times to do the trick to be sure it works, though, and computer scientists (if not magicians) are naturally lazy. Why do more work than needed? Let's do some more reasoning. We can make a simplified picture of the pack and look at what happens as we throw away every second card. In doing this, we are creating a *model* of the pack of cards. This kind of **computational modelling** is an important part of computational thinking. We represent each card by it's position in the pack at the start as we suggested. We will use "..." to show the numbers could go further or even not as far (more **abstraction**). This is our model of the pack:

1 2 3 4 5 6 7 8 9 10 11 12 13 14 15 16 17 18 19 ...

What are we left with if we discard every second card starting from the first? Just the even numbered positions are left and that means the 16th card is left in the pack:

2 4 6 8 10 12 14 16 18 ...

We can keep discarding every second card leaving positions:

4 8 12 16 ...

and then

8 16

and finally

16.

We can see from the model that the same thing will happen even if there were more or less cards. We are apparently left with the 16th card every time, just by crossing out every second card.

There is a problem though and it is in the "...".s. This is an important point about **abstraction**. If you abstract away important detail, you can get the wrong answer to the problem you were trying to solve. **Logical thinking** can also easily lead you astray if you don't manage to think very precisely about every alternative that is possible. If we had split the pack before the 16th card at the start, then the 16th card would not have been left as it would of course already have been removed in that first cut. Then we would have ended up with a different card such as the eighth card. You may have realised that earlier, as soon as we started abstracting the problem. There is another similar, slightly more subtle problem though. Let's do the modelling again with a bigger model. The result is Figure 7.

Oops. With 32 or more cards at the start, we would end up with the 32nd card not the 16th. Therefore, even if we make sure the 16th card isn't discarded at the start, our trick still doesn't always work if done naively. We have to add another proviso. For our trick to work, our logical argument shows the cut must be made after the 16th card and before the 32nd. That's why it's important that you tell the volunteer you need to discard "roughly half" the pack. However, you don't really mean roughly half, you mean very precisely "somewhere between the 16th and 32nd card". That is why you spread your hands, placing them over the 16th and 32nd cards, as the volunteer points to a card. It is to make sure the *proviso*, or *precondition* as a programmer would call it, holds true without the volunteer realising what you are doing.

So, we have used **computational modelling** with **logical thinking** to show that the trick does work: but only if there are at least 16 and not more than 31 cards in the pile when you start the deal. Computational modelling involves making models of

1 2 3 4 5 6 7 8 9 10 11 12 13 14 15 16 ... 25 26 27 28 29 30 31 32 33 34 35 36 ...
2 4 6 8 10 12 14 16 18 20 22 24 26 28 30 32 34 36 ...
4 8 12 16 20 24 28 32 36 ...
8 16 24 32 ...
16 32 ...
32

Figure 7: A model of discarding cards if we start with more than 32 cards.

a computational process to explore it. Here we did it to explore whether the trick always worked, but a similar idea can be useful in generalising a trick too. Our model gives the essence of what makes the trick work. It is not about playing cards really. Our model abstracted them away along with lots of other detail. In doing this, we might start thinking about other presentations of the trick based on that raw essence of what makes the trick work. We will return to that.

Punch Cards

The magic of finding things

This trick has a deeper link to computing algorithms than just the point that both tricks and programs are algorithms. A version of the trick's algorithm is actually the basis of a way early computers could search through data stored on punch cards. Punch cards are physical cards that were used as long-term memory for early computers: a place where data to be processed could be saved.

Information was put on a punch card by punching holes into it in special patterns: using a code a bit like a spy's code. Spies might use arcane symbols for their codes, computers used a code of holes and no-holes. Unlike a spy's secret code, with computer codes, the idea is that the meaning of the symbols is well known to anyone interested. The specific code computers still use for simple numbers is called *binary*.

Figure 8 gives an example punch card for the number 22. To see how punch cards can be used to search for data using the magic down-under deal, first you need to make yourself a set of cards. We will then explain how they work.

You can download templates to print out from the website: www.cs4fn.org/punchcards/

Print them out, ideally directly on to thin card. Sprinkling talcum powder on the cards will stop them sticking together (and it is important they don't stick).

Rather than using holes and no-holes, for our code, we will use holes and notches. You must cut out the right notches to match the number of the card. The small numbers under the notches must add

Figure 8: A punch card for the number 22 i.e., $16 + 0 + 4 + 2 + 0$.

up to the big number on the card. For example, the card, 22, has notches against 16, 4 and 2, and $16 + 4 + 2 = 22$. To understand what is going on here, we need to understand some simple maths: the binary code we are using ...

Touching Bases

Binary is just a different way to write numbers, but one where you are only allowed to use the digits 0 and 1 rather than all the digits 0, 1, 2, 3, 4, 5, 6, 7, 8 and 9 as we normally do. Our normal number system is called base-10. The base tells us how many different digits (different symbols) that we have available. Binary is base-2: we just have two digits available. On our punch cards, we are going to use holes for 0 and slots for 1. Binary and base-10 are just two different ways to represent numbers. Choosing a good **representation** for information is another important part of computational thinking.

Let's look at base-10 first so we can then compare it to binary. In base-10, we use the digits to count up to 9 but then run out of digits so at that point have to use a new column. We go back to 0 but carry 1 into the next column where that 1 now stands for 10 as shown in Figure 9.

Any digit in the second column stands for 10 times as much as the same digit in the first column. In base-10, the number 16 is one

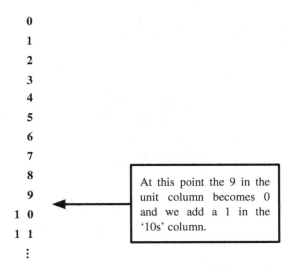

Figure 9: Counting in decimal.

lot of 10 (a 1 in the 10s column) and then six units (a 6 in the 1s column). We add 10 and 6 to get the number 16. Similarly, 987 means 9 lots of 100, 8 lots of 10, and 7 1s are added together.

100	10	1	×	
9	8	7	=	
900 +	80 +	7	=	987

Binary works in just the same way except that we run out of digits earlier. We have to use a new column when we get to 1, rather than going all the way up to 9 (see Figure 10). Instead of 1s, 10 and 100s, that means the columns now stand for 1s, 2s, 4s, 8s and so on.

This means we write the number 5, for example, in binary (so using only digits 1 and 0) as 101. It is 1 lot of 4 plus 0 lots of 2 plus 1 unit.

If we show 5 columns of digits (as we will on our punch cards) then 5 in binary is 00101.

16	8	4	2	1	×	
0	0	1	0	1	=	
0 +	0 +	4 +	0 +	1	=	5

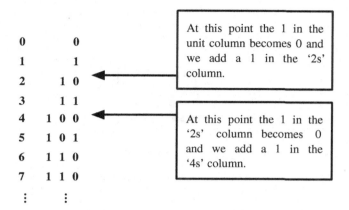

Figure 10: Counting in binary.

Similarly, 16 in binary is 10000.

16	8	4	2	1	×	
1	0	0	0	0	=	
16 +	0 +	0 +	0 +	0	=	16

Notice that, apart from the units column, all the other powers of two that make up the binary number columns are even. As we are adding numbers, the only way an odd number can be represented in binary is if there is a 1 in the unit column. All odd numbers have a 1 there, and even numbers don't. That will be important later.

Binary punch cards

What does this have to do with our punch cards? Well, we can store binary numbers on cards using holes for 0 and slots for 1. To put the number 5 onto a punch card, starting from the left, we need a hole (0), then another hole (0), then a slot (1), a hole (0) and finally a slot (1). For the number 16 (10000), we need a slot then the rest holes. With space for five holes, we can store any number up to 31 on a card. With enough space (i.e., enough powers of two and so digits) we could store any number like this. The corresponding punch cards are given in Figures 11(a) and 11(b).

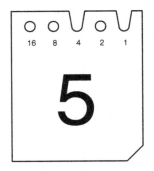

(a) A punch card for the number 5
i.e., $0 + 0 + 4 + 0 + 1$

(b) A punch card for the number 16
i.e., $16 + 0 + 0 + 0 + 0$

Figure 11: Example punch cards demonstrating the binary coding.

Once we've stored a number on to a card in binary as holes and slots, we can then easily find any individual card we want. That is where the down-under deal comes in.

Take the stack of cards and make sure they are all the same way round with the cut off corner in the same place and holes lined up. Now put a pencil through the rightmost hole (the units column), and shake out all the cards with a slot in that position. All those with a 1 in the binary at that position fall out (remember that's the odd numbers), leaving only those with a 0. Now go back to the binary number of the card you are trying to find. If there is a 0 in its binary at that position, then *discard* the down pile: the cards that shake out. If there is a 1 in that position of the binary in the target number, then *keep* the down pile. Do the same for each hole in turn.

Let's look at an example: finding card 16. In binary, it is 10000. From the right that becomes:

SLOT 1: 0 — DISCARD those that fall
SLOT 2: 0 — DISCARD those that fall
SLOT 4: 0 — DISCARD those that fall
SLOT 8: 0 — DISCARD those that fall
SLOT 16: 1 — KEEP those that fall

Repeatedly discard the down pile until, on the fifth round, you keep the down pile. It will be card 16. It's actually possible to find any card, just by spelling out the binary like that. Try and find card 5. In binary, it is 00101. From the right that becomes

SLOT 1: 1 — KEEP those that fall
SLOT 2: 0 — DISCARD those that fall
SLOT 4: 1 — KEEP those that fall
SLOT 8: 0 — DISCARD those that fall
SLOT 16: 0 — DISCARD those that fall

You will be left holding card 5.

So, How Does That Work?

It turns out that what is happening as you shake out the cards is exactly the same thing as in the down-under deal. To see this, we just need a little bit more **logical thinking** to come up with a rigorous argument about what is happening.

Take the first round, discarding cards when looking for the number 16. Shaking out those first punch cards and then getting rid of them throws away all cards that have a slot (a 1) in the first position of the binary number. That is the unit column. The numbers 1, 3, 5, 7 and so on have a slot (a 1) in that position: it's all the odd numbers. It's the same as in the first round of the down-under deal where we throw away alternate cards. As we saw earlier, you work out what a binary number stands for by adding up the contribution to the number of the separate digits (like $5 = 4 + 0 + 1$). That last unit digit is the only way to make odd numbers as all the other digits represent even numbers (2, 4, 8, 16, ...)

Here is another way to think about why the binary version leads to the odd ones being thrown out that will help us see later why the rest of the trick works. Think about the way that we count in binary. 0, 1, 2, 3, 4, ... is in binary: 000, 001, 010, 011, 100, ... That unit column flips every second number as we count i.e., that last position in the number counts 0, 1, 0, 1 and so on. This means that if we throw away all the 1s, then we are throwing away every second card.

So we have shown that in round one, the same thing happens as in the trick. Having taken out all the odd numbered cards we move on to the next hole on the punch cards and so the next position in the binary number. That shakes out all the numbers that include 2 in the addition making up the number. For example, 6 is one of them. It is 110 in binary because $6 = 4 + 2 + 0$. The numbers dropping out this time are 2 (10 in binary), 3 (11 in binary), 6 (110), 7 (111), 10 (1010 in binary), 11 (1011 in binary) and so on. The odd numbers have already been removed though, so the ones left that are shaken out this time are 2, 6, 10, ... That is every second card that is left. It is the same sequence of cards as are removed in the second round of the down-under deal.

We can, again, see why if we think of the way the binary counting system works on the second column. It counts 0, 0, 1, 1, 0, 0, 1, 1, 0, 0, 1, 1 ... You can see this pattern in the middle column of the following sequence for three digit binary numbers.

0	0 **0** 0
1	0 **0** 1
2	0 **1** 0
3	0 **1** 1
4	1 **0** 0
5	1 **0** 1
6	1 **1** 0
7	1 **1** 1

It happens because in binary, the second digit only changes when the first binary digit has counted twice (0, 1) itself. Now, if we have already removed every second card of that sequence we are left not with the sequence 0, 0, 1, 1, 0, 0, 1, 1, 0, 0, 1, 1 ... but 0, 1, 0, 1, 0, 1, ... That leaves us with:

0	0 **0** 0
2	0 **1** 0
4	1 **0** 0
6	1 **1** 0

Given the punch cards left at this point, we are actually doing the same as in the first round: discarding all the 1s mean discarding every second punch card, because the middle 1s are every second punch card in the above sequence.

The same thing happens on every round of removing cards. We are actually shaking out every second card that is left every time. The difference to the trick is that the numbers on the punch card don't refer to the card's position but to its binary hole and slot label. That means they can be shuffled and we still find the card. Another difference is that with the punch cards all the cards are removed in one go: in parallel. Whereas the down-under deal was very slow and boring as we went through every card in turn, the punch card version is very fast.

In computer science terms, the card trick uses a *sequential algorithm*: we do one thing at a time, move one card at a time. Most computer programs are written like that: their instructions are followed one after the other. The punch card searching is an example of a *parallel algorithm*. Rather than doing one thing at a time, on some steps at least, we do lots of things at once, shaking out lots of cards. That means while the playing card deal is really slow, the punch card version is fast. Parallel algorithms are the future of programming. With each new generation of technology, more processors become available in both computers and the other gadgets around us, as the technology for making them improves. This involves what are called *multicore* chips: lots of computers on a chip. We can also create even bigger networks of computers that can work effectively together on single problems. This means the way to do things more efficiently is to design our algorithms so that every processor available always has something useful to do. We need parallel algorithms.

Another reason that the punch card algorithm is fast is because it uses a *divide and conquer* approach to solve the problem of finding things. It is similar to the one we saw in the previous chapter. In fact, with a bit of **generalisation**, we are still actually talking about search algorithms. We are searching for a playing card and searching for a punch card. Divide and conquer is a general way of solving problems really quickly though so it is useful in other situations that aren't about searching too. As we saw, the secret behind divide and conquer is to repeatedly halve the size of the problem. What does that mean for our cards? On each round we remove half of the cards that remain. How do we search those left? We do the same again, removing half, and then half again, and so on. The halving here is based on the binary representation, though, rather than simply the first or second half.

Having realised this is just a search problem we can immediately see other ways we could search for a punch card: the solutions we saw in the previous chapter all work. The simplest is to check each card in turn to see if it is the one we are looking for: *linear search.* Our divide and conquer algorithm is much faster, precisely because it cuts the size of the problem in half on every step. If the cards were sorted, we could use *binary search* to find the one we wanted. That is fast though our new version is better in this situation as it is not only fast, it works even when the punch cards are shuffled.

Inventing New Tricks (Again)

New tricks from old

Tricks can be invented in a similar way to the way programmers write programs. Programmers normally don't start from nothing. They often adapt parts of an existing program that does something similar. In the same way, rather than starting completely with a blank piece of paper, one way to invent a new trick is to start with one that already works and adapt it until it becomes something different. The same core algorithm can be adapted to different purposes. This is **generalisation** in action again. The magician takes the core idea in an existing trick and generalises it.

It may also be possible to create a new twist on an old trick by combining a series of old steps from different tricks. The idea here is to use **decomposition**. By chaining a series of effects together, you may end up with something even more magical. For example, if you know a way to do a false shuffle, where you pretend to shuffle the pack, but can leave the middle cards in the same position at the end of the shuffle, then combining that with this trick makes something even more magical.

A third way is to adapt the presentation. Once you have developed an underlying mechanism that makes the foundation of a good trick, you can reuse it with completely different presentations. You can turn it into a different version of the trick. You might do this just by telling a different story around the same algorithm, or do more major changes as we will see.

New tricks from computing

We've seen that self-working tricks and computer programs are essentially the same thing. Some tricks involve exactly the same algorithms as are used by computers such as we saw here for searching. That means we can do some more **generalisation**, more sharing of solutions. In the trick we had to find the 16th card, but we saw with the punch cards we can end up with any card at all just by spelling out the binary to decide which pile to keep. So we could take that idea back into the world of magic. You could invent a version of the trick that involves planting the card anywhere at the start. It doesn't have to be the 16th card! You must of course know exactly where it has been placed. You also need to be able to do the binary in your head. Being good at mental maths is a useful skill for a magician as well as a computer scientist!

However, you can go a step further than just doing a slight modification to the trick like this. If you can **abstract** what is happening down to the mathematical pattern behind the algorithm, what the effect is rather than the steps to achieve it, then you can end up with a completely different trick too.

Pick a pile

Let's see how this might work for the Australian Magician's Dream. It works, as we saw with the punch cards, because on each step we either discard or keep a collection of numbers based on their binary representation. The first round removes the odd numbered punch cards. They are the ones with a 1 in the first position of their binary (the 1s column): 1, 3, 5, 7, ... (0001, 0011, 0101, 0111, ...). On the next round, we lose those numbered 2, 6, ... Those are the cards with a 1 in the second position of the binary (the 2s column) i.e., 0010, 0110, ... That isn't all the cards with a 1 there in the binary as some have gone already as we saw. So let's list all the cards with a 1 in that position. That gives the longer list of 2, 3, 6, 7, 10, ... (0010, 0011, 0110, 1111, 1010, ...). The next deal got rid of numbered cards with a 1 in the third position of the binary (the 4's column). The full list of those is 4, 5, 6, 7, 12, ... (0100, 0101, 0110, 0111, 1100 ...). Now, notice that there is another pattern here. The first number in each list tells you the column of the binary it is the list for.

So here is a different trick based on that pattern. Make a pile of cards with the numbers 1, 3, 5, 7, 9, 11, 13, 15 written on them. Make a second pile of cards with the numbers: 2, 3, 6, 7, 10, 11, 14, 15 written on them. Make a third pile: 4, 5, 6, 7, 12, 13, 14, 15. Finally, make a fourth row with 8, 9, 10, 11, 12, 13, 14, 15. Shuffle the cards in each pile. The piles can also be in any order.

Now ask a volunteer to think of a number between 1 and 15, and remember it. They should not tell you what it is. Take one of the piles and deal the cards one at a time on to the table. Explain that you are able to read their mind as they look at the cards, even without looking at them, just at the cards. Ask the volunteer when you finish dealing the pile out to tell you if their number was in the pile, as an extra "lie detector test" to help you calibrate against their thoughts. If they say the number was there, then set the cards aside. If not put them back. Do this with each pile.

After the fourth pile, tell them the number they were thinking of! How do you do it?

You just need to remember the smallest number in each pile that is set aside. Add them up and you have the number the person was thinking of. Why? Those lowest numbers are the numbers that represent the binary digit that is in all the cards in that pile. If the pile is discarded, then the mystery number has that digit set to 1 in its binary. Add up the different values and you are just converting the binary back to decimal. For example, if they discard the 1 pile and the 4 pile, they are telling you the number is 0101 in binary, so 5 in decimal ($0\times8 + 1\times4 + 0\times2 + 1\times1 = 4 + 1 = 5$).

You have a new trick based on the same underlying mathematical pattern as the old one.

Magicians note

The 16th card principle seems to have originated in 1958 from computer programmer and famous magician *Alex Elmsley* in a trick "7–16" in the magic magazine, *Ibidem*. Alex Elmsley is probably most famous amongst magicians for his card counting sleight of hand technique named after him, the Elmsley count.

From tricks to programs and back

So, understanding computer science and the mathematical patterns behind it can lead to new tricks. The opposite in fact is also true. There is a history of magicians coming up with new computing innovations based on their tricks. People who invent new tricks are doing the same thing as those inventing algorithms for computers, writing new programs. You may have heard that expert programmers are often called 'wizards'. Programmers really are wizards!

Chapter 4

Puzzles, Logic and Patterns

How do we solve logic puzzles? Logical thinking is obviously a core part of doing puzzles, but generalisation and pattern matching are the secret skills of experts. They are used in solving puzzles, in doing computer science, and in many other areas too, from playing chess to fighting fires. Logical thinking, generalisation and pattern matching are all central to computational thinking, too.

Cut Hive Puzzles

Logic puzzles

If you enjoy logic puzzles, and are good at them, you will probably enjoy computer science too. Above anything else, being able to think logically is important to computer scientists. It runs through the whole subject, but is especially important in writing programs. Programs are founded on logic, and as we have already seen, thinking clearly through all the possibilities is important for writing correct programs (and magic tricks). Programs have to work under all circumstances, so when both writing them and evaluating them, the programmer has to sweat the detail.

At one level, when we talk about **logical thinking**, we just mean thinking clearly, chasing down the small details. However, there is a deeper meaning: that of working with mathematical logic, and if you can do that you will be much, much stronger at arguing cast iron cases. It is all about applying rules precisely. Arguments founded on logic have no-holes in them: something that the ancient Greek philosophers realised was an important skill. Being able to come up with solid arguments is useful whatever you do, not just for computer scientists. Logic puzzles are really about constructing an argument, but cut down to the pure logic. Thinking logically is just a skill like any other that can be learnt and improved. It just takes practice (lots of it as with any other skill), and doing puzzles is a fun way to do that practice. The more you do it the more you will develop computational thinking tricks to do it even better.

Cut hives

There are a lot of different kinds of logic puzzles, and they all rely on the same ability to think logically. You've probably seen Sudoku in puzzle books or paper: logic puzzles based on a grid of numbers. Let's explore logical thinking using a simpler kind of logic puzzle, called Cut Hive puzzles. They are inspired by the Cut Block puzzles of Japanese puzzle inventor, *Naoki Inaba*.

A Cut Hive puzzle consists of a block of hexagons: the hive. Areas of the hive are marked out using thicker lines. There are two rules that must hold of a completed hive.

1. Each marked out area must contain the numbers from 1 up to the number of hexagons in the area. For example, the topmost area in the puzzle in Figure 12 consists of four hexagons, so those hexagons must be filled with the numbers: 1, 2, 3 and 4. No numbers should be repeated. If the area has two hexagons, like the one bottom left in the figure, then it must be filled with the numbers 1 and 2.

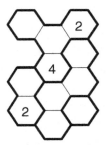

Figure 12: A simple cut hive puzzle.

2. No number can be next to the same number, in any direction along a shared edge. So in the hive of Figure 12, the fact that there is a 4 in the middle hexagon means there cannot be a 4 in any of the five hexagons surrounding it.

Figure 12 is a simple Cut Hive Puzzle for you to solve. Try to complete it before you read on.

Solving a cut hive

Here is the logical reasoning I used to complete the puzzle. My reasoning is based on the rules together with the shape of the hive and the starting numbers given. It is an argument that the filled out grid that I am claiming is a solution, really is a solution.

At the bottom right of the grid is an area containing a single cell. That area has one hexagon so, by the first rule, must contain the numbers from 1 up to ... well 1. That means it must be 1 as in Figure 13.

Next, at the bottom left, we have an area of two hexagons. It must contain the numbers 1 and 2 (by the first rule). One hexagon already has a number 2 in it, so the only possibility left for the other hexagon is 1 (see Figure 14).

The remaining two areas are made of four hexagons each. We now have to be a bit cleverer than so far. Look at the 1 in the bottom corner. The fact that it is a 1 means none of the three hexagons round it can be a 1 (by the second rule). However, that area has only four hexagons in it and one of them must be a 1 (by the first rule). That

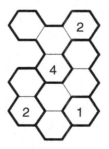

Figure 13: The single cell must be 1.

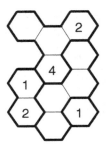

Figure 14: The other number in the pair of hexagons must be 1.

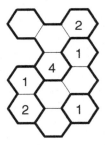

Figure 15: In the lower group of four hexagons only the top-most hexagon can be a 1.

means the last hexagon in the area that isn't next to the 1 must be the 1 because there isn't anywhere else for it to go. We get the hive of Figure 15.

Next we can try and work out where the 2 goes in that same area. There is a 2 that touches both the lower two hexagons, leaving the hexagon sandwiched between the two 1s down the right side as the only possibility for the 2 (see Figure 16).

There is also a 4 above that area and the new 4 can't be next to it. It must be at the bottom. That determines which way round the 3 and 4 must be in the remaining two hexagons as shown in Figure 17.

We are now left with the top area. We can fill it in using similar reasoning. The 1 in the adjacent area means there is only one possible place for the last 1 to go in the top left corner as in Figure 18.

That means the final hexagon is a 3 as that area must have numbers 1–4 and only the 3 is missing. The full solution is given in Figure 19.

Figure 16: The lower two hexagons are touching a 2, so the 2 must be in the other free hexagon.

Figure 17: Because of the 4 in the middle, the next 4 must go at the bottom, leaving the last hexagon as a 3.

Figure 18: Because of the 1 on the side, the remaining 1 must go at the far corner from it.

We have solved the puzzle. We did it by applying the two rules and our basic facts of which numbers were already known. From them, we repeatedly worked out new facts about the puzzle. We've been using a particular kind of logical reasoning called

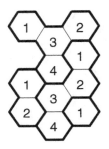

Figure 19: The solution to the cut hive puzzle.

deduction where we work from known facts and the rules of the world (here the puzzle) to give us new facts. It is essentially the way Sherlock Holmes supposedly worked his detective miracles. He noticed things about people and situations, then deduced new facts that follow from them as a consequence. The more facts he learnt the more he could then go on to deduce, ultimately allowing him to solve crimes. Computer scientists and mathematicians use similar reasoning. Good programmers use exactly this kind of reasoning to convince themselves that their programs work, always.

Deriving Rules

Matching patterns, creating rules

So far, we have been deducing facts directly from the two rules. As you do more puzzles, and get more experience though, you start to solve puzzles in a different way. You start to use some of your natural computational thinking skills: **pattern matching** against situations you have seen before, for example. That lets you solve puzzles faster and with less thought. A further step is to do **generalisation**, widening the situations you pattern match against, rather than them having to be exactly the same. With experience, you start to create new, quicker and very general rules to use. They allow you to do logical reasoning at a higher level, based on these more powerful rules. It's possible because of using **logical thinking**, not directly to solve the puzzle as we've done so far, but to create the new rules. That way you are still sure that they are guaranteed to follow from the basic ones. Let's see what we mean with some examples.

The single hexagon rule

Going back to the way we solved the puzzle above, we worked out that when we have an area consisting of a single hexagon, it must contain the number 1. It follows directly from the first rule. Having realised that, we don't have to think it through again, we can just treat it as a new rule derived from the original.

> 3. **IF** an area has only one hexagon
> **THEN** that hexagon holds the number 1

We can draw a diagram to represent the rule rather than just use words (see Figure 20). We use an arrow to show the change we make to the hive. On the left-hand side, we draw the position we pattern match against and on the right-hand side what we change it to if we find a match. Rules like this are called *production rules, inference rules* or *rewrite rules*. This diagrammatic rule says that if we find an empty area of size one, then we can transform it to a hexagon with 1 in it.

We can now just apply this rule directly without ever thinking about why it holds. Our logical thinking can now work at a higher level at least in this simple situation.

The two hexagon rule

We can create another new rule for areas consisting of two hexagons. We saw that if we have an area of size two, with one hexagon filled with a 2 then the other hexagon must be 1 (see Figure 21).

We can treat this as a **generalised** rule from the actual example in our puzzle. It doesn't matter which hexagon holds the 2, the same

Figure 20: The single hexagon rule.

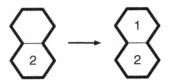

Figure 21: A simple two hexagon rule, where a hexagon holds 2.

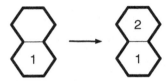

Figure 22: A simple two hexagon rule, where a hexagon holds 1.

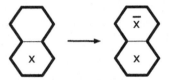

Figure 23: The generalised two hexagon rule.

logic applies. Our picture applies upside down! It can also be applied if the hexagons are linked diagonally in any direction as well.

We can generalise the rule even further. By the same reasoning, if an area of size two has a 1 already placed, then the other hexagon must be 2. This is shown in Figure 22.

Combining these two separate rules gives us the full generalised rule:

4. **IF** a hexagon in an area of size two holds a 1 or a 2
   THEN the other hexagon holds the other number.

We can give it as a diagram if we use a letter x to represent any number (just as mathematicians use x and y as variables in algebra). An x can stand for 1 one time we use the rule, and as a 2 another time, as long as it doesn't change in the middle of any particular time we apply it. A diagram of the rule is given in Figure 23. We use

$\bar{x}$ in the diagram to mean the other number. So if x is 1, then $\bar{x}$ is 2, and if x is 2, then $\bar{x}$ is 1. This rule can match an area of size two rotated in any way and so whichever way round the two numbers are. This diagram turns into our original rules (and their diagrams) just by setting x to 1 or 2. We are starting to invent a mathematical-like notation for the same reason mathematicians use symbols. It gives us a precise way to talk about things, and as our rules become more complicated that is important if we aren't going to make mistakes.

Rather than deducing facts from given facts using the original rules for the puzzle, we are now deducing new 'bigger' rules that hold given those original rules. These are called *derived inference rules*. Whenever we see a situation that matches the pattern of one of our new rules, we don't have to think any more about why it is true, we can just apply the rule. We have **abstracted** away from the reason the rule holds.

The corner rule

Let's look at a final example of creating a bigger rule from our solution to the simple cut hive puzzle that turns out to be quite useful. In the bottom right corner, we were able to deduce where the next 1 in the area of four hexagons should go. It was possible because there was already a 1 in the adjacent area, nestled into a corner as in Figure 24.

There must be a 1 in position a, b, c or d of Figure 24. However, there can't be a 1 next to another 1 by the second rule of the puzzle.

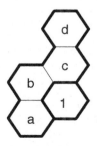

Figure 24: A 1 surrounded by hexagons on one side.

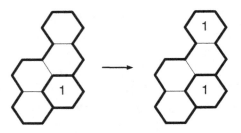

Figure 25: A simple corner rule.

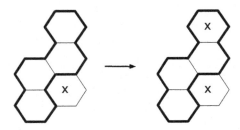

Figure 26: A generalised corner rule.

That rules out positions a, b and c. The 1 must be in position d as it is all that is left. We can draw that step as a rewrite rule diagram (see Figure 25).

Of course, any of the hexagons shown as blank could already be filled with other numbers and the rule will still apply: that is another way of **generalising** our new rule. Also, as before, the number we are pattern matching against doesn't have to be a 1. It could be any number formed as part of a bigger area. If we use a letter x again to represent any number, then our rule becomes the generalised version of Figure 26.

We can even generalise our rule in a further way. The area we are filling doesn't have to be exactly that shape. The extra hexagon could be in any position round the far edge of the bigger area: anywhere that is connected but doesn't touch the corner hexagon. In the version of the corner rule in Figure 27, we've used question marks to act as variables that show the possible positions of the hexagon of interest.

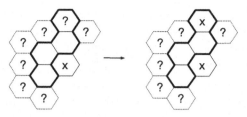

Figure 27: A corner rule generalised over the position of the hexagon being filled.

Written in English, we get a generalised rule:

5. **IF** a hexagon is next to an area of size four, with only three of the four hexagons touching it
THEN the fourth hexagon holds the same number as the surrounded hexagon.

As before, the rule will apply upside down or on its side, rotated or reflected. Perhaps you can think of even more ways to **generalise** the rule.

Equipped now with this very general rule, if you find any situation that you can pattern match it against in a puzzle, then you can apply it. You can fill in a missing number, as indicated by whatever matches the x.

Writing rules down

Most people who do puzzles don't bother to write down the rules they derive and use. They just remember something that worked in the past and apply it when the chance arises, without much thought. Computer Scientists like to write things like that down though. Why is it a good idea? The reasons are similar to those for writing down algorithms. For one thing you can use them to teach other people how to do the puzzles without them having to work it all out for themselves (as we just did for you). The rules can even be used to teach computers how to do the puzzles. It also makes things precise. It is easy to have a false recollection of a rule that worked in the past, or for someone who has learnt it to misunderstand the detail. In either case, it could lead to the rule being applied incorrectly, or applied to a new situation that it doesn't actually quite match. Writing a precise version down helps avoid this kind of faulty reasoning.

We are stretching the limits of what we can do with pictures now, though. In reality, computer scientists tend to use mathematical notation (called *formal logic*) to express rules. These languages for expressing logic are a bit like programming languages though very flexible. They have the big advantage that they can easily be processed by computers and so be the basis of computers doing this kind of reasoning. The logic becomes the basis for computer programs that can solve the puzzles.

Many Artificial Intelligence systems are based on the idea of programming using this kind of *production rule*. Instead of drawing diagrams, we write rules of the form

IF <some situation> **THEN** <action to do>

A list of such rules makes a program. If a rule applies, then the computer can do the action. If several apply, it just picks any to apply. This is done over and over again. This gives a different paradigm for writing programs: a whole new way of thinking about what a program is, rather than just a sequence of commands that are followed as we've talked about so far.

We aren't just using **logical thinking** as we become better and better at doing the puzzles. We **pattern match** the rules against the current situation to know which to apply. A production rule-based program is doing the same kind of pattern matching. It is doing some simple computational thinking!

In writing the rules down to create that program, **generalisation** goes hand in hand with **abstraction**: we are hiding detail about other parts of the puzzle to make things easier to think about and to make the rules as general as possible. In the diagram for our last rule, we have used several abstractions to describe what we can **pattern match** against. For example, the variable x is an **abstraction**. It abstracts away from (i.e., hides the detail of) the actual number involved: we can apply it whatever the number. Similarly we have abstracted away from the details of the area that already has a number. We are also using question marks as another kind of variable to abstract away from the position of the fourth hexagon in our

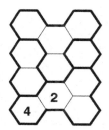

Figure 28: A second simple cut hive puzzle.

representation of the rule. We have also abstracted away from the orientation in the way we write the rule: the diagram can be rotated or reflected in any way to match a puzzle state.

More Puzzles

Another simple puzzle

Figure 28 is a new puzzle to try. See if you can use any of our rules above to solve it. As you fill in numbers you will find that new rules apply. If none of our derived rules applies, you might have to go back to the original puzzle rules. Remember that the second rule says that a number can't be next to itself. The answer is at the end of the chapter.

A harder puzzle

Figure 29 is another, much bigger, harder puzzle. As you solve it, look out for other rules you might devise, either that are immediately useful again in solving this puzzle, or that might be useful for future puzzles.

HINT: In looking for a new rule, think about what happens when you have lines of areas of size three next to one another.

Logical Thinking and Expertise

Logical thinking matters

Why does **logical thinking** matter to a computer scientist? Because it is at the subject's heart. Computers work based on logic, so to be

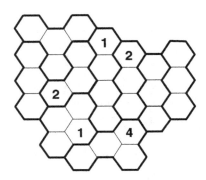

Figure 29: A harder cut hive puzzle.

able to program them, to give them instructions, you have to think logically as well. Otherwise, you are likely to make mistakes.

Logical thinking is a key part of computational thinking that runs through all aspects of it, whether the task in hand is to create algorithms or evaluate them. Programmers need to think logically when developing a new program, when modifying an existing program to do something new, when looking for bugs in their programs, and when evaluating them in other ways.

Logics themselves are very simple and precise mathematical languages. Like our puzzles, logics come with a set of rules, called their *axioms*. Our initial two rules of the puzzle are its axioms. From axioms, mathematicians derive higher level rules, just as we did, allowing them to reason in large steps.

Such logics form the foundation of programming languages, defining what each construct in the language means, so those designing programming languages have to think logically too. Having logic as the basis of programming languages is the reason we can use logical thinking to reason about what our programs do. We can even prove programs are correct. To make that possible, computer scientists also write descriptions of what a program should do directly in logic. Then the logical reasoning is used to show that the program's logical effect is equivalent to that of the description of what it should do.

As we also saw Computer Scientists have even invented ways that logical rules can be treated directly as programs themselves.

In this style of programming, called *Logic Programming*, writing a program involves coming up with rules that when applied do some computation. Our rules for the puzzle, written in a logic programming language would become a program for solving the puzzles. Whatever kind of language you program in, though you have to apply logical thinking, one way or another.

Experts at work

The more experience we get of doing puzzles, the more rules we mentally accumulate and the faster, more easily we can do new puzzles. This is the way that chess grand masters play chess too. They recognise positions of the game as being similar to situations they have seen before. They then make moves that their experience suggests will be a good move. By thinking that way, they avoid having to think through vast numbers of moves ahead, which is slow and error-prone for a human. Computers on the other hand do play like that, playing out lots of alternative moves and seeing the consequences. Human chess players are geniuses at the game because they are using both **logical thinking** and **pattern matching**, and have built up a wealth of informal rules about the game.

It isn't just expert chess players that think like that. It has been suggested that pretty well all experts work the same way, whatever skill they are an expert at. Fire fighters, for example, do the same. When they have a hunch that a situation is bad and get out of a burning building just before the roof collapses, it is similar to **pattern matching** that is going on, but sub-consciously. Intuition is just sub-conscious **pattern matching** against lots of prior experience.

If you want to be an expert at anything, develop your **pattern matching** and **generalisation** skills. For any skill, to be considered a genius at it and be stunningly successful, there is a rule of thumb that you need to put in 10,000 hours of practice. Virtuoso violinists, for example, will have practised playing the violin at least that long. Similarly, the most successful programmers, the ones who have become billionaires, practised writing programs for around 10,000 hours. Even Tibetan monks who are renowned for their serenity, inner peace and compassion will have practised meditation to gain that inner peace for at least the same length of time.

If you want to be a great computer scientist, start practising your computational thinking skills now. Even if you don't want to be a programmer, developing the skills like **logical thinking**, **generalisation**, **abstraction** and **pattern matching** will make you better at whatever career you follow, whatever you want to be an expert at. Doing logic puzzles is a fun way to develop them, especially if you think about how you are solving the puzzles as you do them, writing down your rules.

Answers

Figures 30 and 31 give the answers to the last two puzzles.

Figure 30: The answer to the second, easy cut hive puzzle.

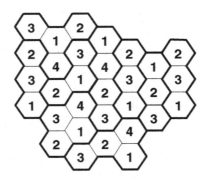

Figure 31: The answer to the harder cut hive puzzle.

Chapter 5

Puzzling Tours

Find a way for a chess knight to visit every square on a board exactly once, solve a problem for a city tour guide, and finish off by advising a tourist information centre. Do all three better as a result of some computational thinking. Oh and help the tourists to pack too. Algorithms are at the heart of computational thinking, allowing us to solve a problem once and then avoid having to think about it ever again. However, choosing a good representation for the information involved is another important part of computational thinking. Do it well and your algorithms will be so much easier to come by.

Two Puzzles

The Knight's Tour puzzle

In the Knight's Tour puzzle, a single chess knight is able to move on a small cross-shaped board. A knight can move two spaces in one direction and then move one square at right angles, or vice versa. It jumps to the new square without visiting any in between, and must always end up on a square on the board. Possible first moves on the knight's tour are shown in Figure 32.

You must find a sequence of moves that starts from square 1, visits every square exactly once by making such knight's moves, and finishes where it started.

Solve it!

Try and solve the Knight's Tour puzzle, timing yourself to see how long it takes you. You must do more than just get the knight to

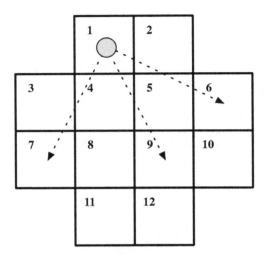

Figure 32: Moves on the knight's tour board.

do a correct tour, though. You must find an algorithmic solution. That means more than just moving the piece around the board. You must record the series of moves that works. That is, you must use algorithmic thinking and come up with an algorithm that solves the puzzle. Your algorithm could just be written as a list of the numbers of the squares to visit in the order they should be visited. Or, you could, for example, write the algorithm as a series of commands like "Move from square 1 to square 9". It's up to you.

Once you have an algorithm that works, evaluate it: double check that it really is a solution by trying it out. Follow your instructions, marking the squares as the knight visits them. That way, you can be sure that it doesn't break the rules: that it visits every square exactly once. If you solve the puzzle, then well done! If you can't, then don't worry: we will see how to make it easier to do later. First let's try an easier puzzle.

The tour guide puzzle

You are a hotel tour guide. Tourists staying in your hotel expect to be taken on a day trip visiting all the city's attractions. You have been given a map (see Figure 33) that shows the locations of

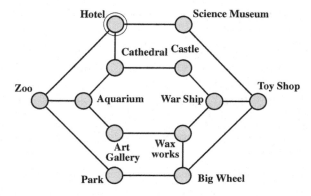

Figure 33: The tour guide's map.

the attractions and how you can get from one to another using the underground network.

You must work out a route that starts from the hotel and will take your tour group to every tourist site. The tourists are only in the city for the day, so don't want to waste time. They will be unhappy if they pass through the same place twice. Obviously, they also want to end up back at their hotel that evening.

As with the Knight's Tour, your task is to come up with an algorithmic solution. Check that your solution does work. How long did it take you? Was it easier (i.e., you solved it faster) than the Knight's Tour?

What's required?

Why is it important that you check that you definitely do have a correct solution? Well, you wouldn't want to actually do the tour and find at the end of the day that you missed something important. You don't want to have to deal with angry tourists!

One way to check an algorithm is to do what computer scientists call *dry running*, or *tracing*, your algorithm. That just means you follow the steps of the algorithm on paper before you do it for real. That is probably how you checked your solution for the Knight's Tour if you came up with one. For the Tour Guide puzzle, you can draw the route on the map as you follow each instruction, ticking each location as you visit it.

Of course, as a real tour guide you wouldn't just rely on checking the route on paper. You would then go out and test it for real too, but it can save a lot of time to check on paper first. Programmers do the same thing. They check their programs work on paper (dry run them) but then also check them for real: *testing*. Just as you did for the puzzle, programmers test their programs to make sure they always work.

We can actually be a bit more precise about our **evaluation**. We can work out exactly what properties matter for us to have a correct solution. If we write a list of those necessary properties, we can then tick them off as we check whether our solution meets them. Computer scientist's call properties like this, *requirements*.

For the Tour Guide puzzle, we need to check our answer against the following requirements.

1. The tour starts at the hotel.
2. It visits every location.
3. It does not pass through a location already visited.
4. It ends at the hotel.

Go back and write a list of requirements for the Knight's Tour puzzle too. Perhaps you can see similarities? We will come back to that.

Why is it easy?

You probably found the Knight's Tour puzzle harder to solve, but actually it doesn't need to be any harder at all. It can be solved really easily if you use some more computational thinking tricks.

Why is the Tour Guide problem easy? The underground map shows the information that matters clearly, ignoring detail that doesn't matter. It is a good **abstraction** of the problem, in that it makes the solution easy to see. Without the map it would have been harder, even if we knew which stations linked to which. The tube map is a special way of representing the information that we know about the problem we have to solve. It is a special kind of diagram called a *graph*. A graph to a computer scientist is a series of circles (we call those the *nodes* of the graph) and lines that join them (the *edges* of the graph). The nodes and edges represent something about the data that we are interested in. The edges show which nodes are linked in the way that matters for the problem. The tourist attractions are presumably linked by roads too, but in different ways. The road graph would be different. That is the graph we would need if we were running a coach tour!

Ignore it!

We are interested in the tourist attractions (our nodes) and which ones are linked to each other by the underground connections (our edges). We aren't interested in anything else about the places, so we ignore everything else. We hide the exact locations, how far they each are apart, road links and a lot more that doesn't matter to our problem of finding an underground route that visits them all. The graph is an **abstraction** of the real city. We hid all the extra detail that we don't need when we created the graph. The graph only shows the information that matters. That makes it much easier to see the information we do need to solve the problem. It is a good **representation** for the problem at hand.

Simplifying things

Graphs are often used to represent information about the connections between things. You will find them on signs at bus stops showing bus routes, on train and underground maps. They are a very good **representation** in situations where you want to find routes from place to place as we did here. The simplified graph makes it easier to find a route than if we had a fully accurate and detailed map, as then the information that mattered would be hard to see amongst all the detail.

Cycles

Computer scientists actually have a special name for this kind of tour of a graph, where you visit every node in a graph exactly once, returning back to the start. They call it a *Hamiltonian cycle*, named after an Irish Physicist, *William Rowan Hamilton*. He invented a puzzle that involved travelling to every corner of a three-dimensional shape called a dodecahedron by travelling along its edges: a Hamiltonian cycle.

Sharing Solutions

Back to the beginning

You may have noticed by now that the Knight's Tour and Tour Guide problems are very similar. If you wrote out the requirements for the Knight's Tour, you may have seen they were essentially the same for both puzzles:

1. The tour starts at a given point.
2. It must visit every point.
3. It must not pass through a point already visited.
4. It must end at the point it started at.

Both puzzles are asking you to find a Hamiltonian cycle! What we have just done is a computational thinking trick. We have **generalised** both problems to be the same kind of problem. We did it by **pattern matching**: seeing the essential similarities. We **abstracted** away detail like whether it is about hotels and tourist attractions; and whether you move using a knight's move or by following a tube line.

So if the reason the Tour Guide problem was easy was that we had a map — we represented the problem as a graph — then why don't we represent the Knight's Tour problem as a graph too?

We need to do a further **abstraction** of the problem. There are two things to realise. First of all, it doesn't actually matter how the board is laid out. We don't care that the squares of the board are squares, for example: they could be any shape and size. Let's draw each square as a small circle instead, just as the tourist attractions were circles on the underground map. They are just nodes of a graph.

Secondly, which squares are actually physically next to one another doesn't actually matter for the puzzle either. The only thing that matters is which ones you can jump between using a knight's move. So let's draw lines between any two circles when you can use a single knight's move to jump between them. That just mirrors the way the underground map shows which attractions can be jumped between using the underground. They are the edges of a graph.

Creating the graph

To create the graph for the Knight's Tour puzzle, move from square to square drawing circles and lines (nodes and edges) as you go. To be sure you don't miss anything, you need to do it in an organised way. Start with square 1. Draw a circle and label it 1. Now from square 1 you can move to square 9, so draw another circle and label it 9, drawing a line between them. From square 9, you can move to square 3 so put a new circle marked 3 and draw a line to it from circle 9.

Keep doing this until you get back to a circle you have already drawn. Then go back one step and try a different trail from that point. If there are no alternatives you haven't already drawn, go back another step and try from there. Keep doing this until you *backtrack* to square 1, and have run out of new trails to follow from there. When you have finished, you have created a map of the Knight's Tour.

Notice that there are only two moves possible from each of the inner three squares so their nodes will each have two edges (i.e., lines) out of them in the finished map. There are three moves possible from all the other squares so their nodes will have three edges out.

Go for depth

This way to explore all the possible moves needed to draw the graph is called *depth-first search* of the graph: we explore paths to their end, for example, following the trail 1 – 9 – 3 – 11 ... to the end, before backing up and trying different paths. An alternative (called *breadth-first search*) involves drawing all the edges from a node and the nodes they lead to, before moving on to a new node. So for breadth-first search, we would draw all the edges from node 1. Then we might draw all the edges from node 9, then all the edges from node 6 and so on. These are two different algorithms for exploring graphs exhaustively: two different *graph traversal algorithms*. Once you have realised a problem can be **represented** as a graph, you can use either of these algorithms as an organised way to explore the graph and so the problem.

Nice and neat

If the drawing you end up with is a bit messy with lots of lines crossing each other, as in Figure 34, you may want to redraw it neatly with no lines crossing. For this graph, it can be done as two linked hexagons one inside the other as in Figure 35.

Once you have drawn, and tidied, the graph, try and solve the Knight's Tour puzzle again. Start at node 1 and follow the lines, noting the nodes you pass through. It should be fairly easy to come up with a solution.

Same problem, same solution

Now look at the tidied version of the graph carefully. We have redrawn it, without changing any of the nodes or edges, so it looks exactly the same as the tube map. The only difference is in the labels

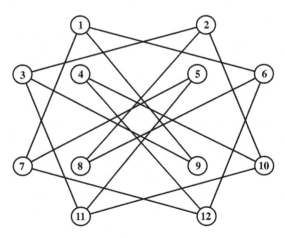

Figure 34: The knight's tour puzzle as a graph.

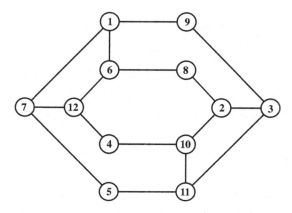

Figure 35: The knight's tour puzzle as a cleaned up graph.

attached to the nodes. They are just numbers instead of names of places.

What this shows is that we can actually **generalise** these two problems to be exactly the same problem, not just the same kind of problem. If you have a solution to one (an algorithm that solves it), then you have a solution to the other immediately too! All you have to do is re-label the graph. A **generalised** version of the algorithm will solve both. You don't actually have to solve it anew.

Mapping between maps

Figure 36 tells you how to re-label a graph describing one of our two problems into a graph describing the other. It also tells you how to convert a solution for one problem into a solution for another. For each step in your answer to one, all you have to do is look it up and swap it for the corresponding label.

So if we came up with the following solution to the Tour Guide:

1. Hotel
2. Science Museum
3. Toy Shop
4. Big Wheel
5. Park
6. Zoo

Knight's Tour Square	Tour Guide Attraction
1	Hotel
2	War ship
3	Toy shop
4	Art gallery
5	Park
6	Cathedral
7	Zoo
8	Castle
9	Science museum
10	Wax works
11	Big wheel
12	Aquarium

Figure 36: Mapping the knight's tour squares to tour guide attractions.

7. Aquarium
8. Art Gallery
9. Wax Works
10. War Ship
11. Castle
12. Cathedral
13. Hotel

then using the table, we immediately get a solution to the Knight's Tour.

1. Square 1
2. Square 9
3. Square 3
4. Square 11
5. Square 5
6. Square 7
7. Square 12

8. Square 4
9. Square 10
10. Square 2
11. Square 8
12. Square 6
13. Square 1

The table is actually another kind of **representation** of information or *data structure* called a *lookup table*. Given a Knight's Tour square, you can easily lookup the equivalent Tour Guide attraction. Though notice that its not quite as convenient for looking up the square that goes with an attraction. It would be easier to do that if it was sorted alphabetically by attraction.

A map for both problems

The map in Figure 37 is another representation of the same information superimposed on the graph. It also shows one solution (to both problems). Of course, as there are multiple solutions possible, the actual solutions you came up with might be different, but if so both solutions will solve both puzzles.

So, perhaps surprisingly, the two apparently different problems are actually exactly the same problem with exactly the same

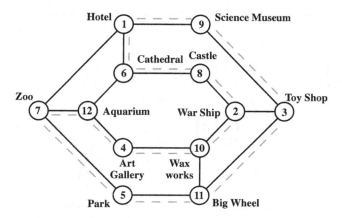

Figure 37: The combined tour guide and knight's tour map showing a solution.

solutions (once **generalised**). Once you have solved one, you have solved both! This insight comes from choosing appropriate **abstractions**, an appropriate **representation** of the two problems (as graph data structures).

The Bridges of Königsberg

Touring a city of bridges

Here is another puzzle to think about. Figure 38 shows a map of the city of Königsberg, showing the river that runs through the middle of the city, its two islands and the seven bridges that cross the river.

The tourist information centre would like to publish a route that visits each part of the city (both banks and both islands) and that crosses each bridge once (and no more). It should start and end in the same place. You have been asked to advise them. Either provide a route or if you can't explain why not.

A variation of this puzzle was solved by the mathematician, *Leonhard Euler*, in the 18th century. His solution introduced the idea of graphs in the first place. This ultimately led to them becoming a key computational thinking tool of both mathematicians and computer scientists. Victorian computer scientists, *Charles Babbage* and *Ada Lovelace*, who wrote the first ever computer programs, are

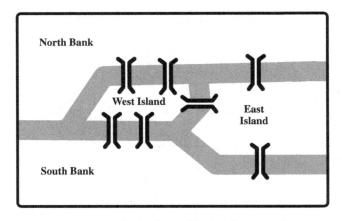

Figure 38: The bridges of Königsberg puzzle.

known to have had a go at solving it in the 19th century. Draw a graph of the problem and see if you can solve it before reading on.

Thinking logically

A core part of computational thinking is being able to think logically. A good representation helps with this by removing the clutter so you can focus on what matters. That is exactly what Leonhard Euler found with the Bridges of Koenigsberg puzzle when he came up with the idea of drawing a graph of the problem (see Figure 39). The graph helped him to do some very clear thinking about the problem.

What he realised looking at the graph was that it was impossible to come up with a route. Why? Any suitable route must visit every node. It must also involve every edge but only once (as the edges are the bridges and we have been told that the route must cross every bridge once). Let's suppose there is such a route and we draw dashed arrows over the edges to show it. All the edges must be on the route so should be dashed. Now think about a node on that route as in Figure 40. It must have a dashed line into it for every dashed line out from it. Otherwise, the route will get stuck when it arrives on that extra non-dashed edge. It will have no way out without going back over a bridge already crossed. The same reasoning applies to every node. That means all nodes must have an even number of edges connected to them for a tour to be possible.

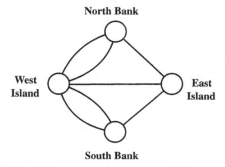

Figure 39: The bridges of Königsberg puzzle as a graph.

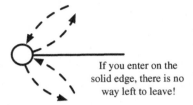

If you enter on the
solid edge, there is no
way left to leave!

Figure 40: Why the bridges of Königsberg puzzle can't be solved.

All the nodes on the Königsberg graph have an odd number of
edges, so there is no such tour possible. Since Euler's time, however,
a new bridge has actually been built over the river in Königsberg,
so the graph is now different. Now tour guides in the city have an
easier life.

Travelling and Packing

Real tours

We've looked at some simple puzzles for finding tours. Now, take a
real problem. Suppose that every day, a sales rep sets her sat nav
the task of plotting the shortest route to visit a series of clients in
different towns just once ending up back at the office and without
doubling back on herself.

It is possible to calculate such a shortest route, but in general
it may be totally impractical to work out the route in a reasonable
amount of time. Even with 20 clients to visit, you just could not
guarantee to find the best solution every day as it would take too
long. It's not about getting a faster sat nav, a faster computer.
Make the number of locations to visit big enough (which is actually
not that big) and it would take longer to get a perfect solution,
than the time that has passed since the universe was created,
even with the fastest conceivable computers! Why? Because the
number of possibilities to check explodes with each extra city to
visit. A sat nav could be programmed to come up with an answer.
It just couldn't be guaranteed to be perfect. The program would

have to do it in a way that sometimes it wouldn't actually give the shortest route possible. It could, for example, use a kind of algorithm called a *greedy algorithm*. Let's change problems to get the idea.

Holiday packing

Suppose you are off on a long relaxing holiday. Your suitcase is open on the bed. You've already packed your clothes in a suitcase and now you are packing others with things to do. You have a pile of things you want to take: books, board games, jigsaws, a pack of cards, painting gear, ... Every relaxing thing you can think of to do. Each thing is a different size. You just have to get them in your suitcases. How do you do it? You could just start trying alternatives. Jigsaw first, then playing cards, a puzzle book and so on. That will work fine if you have plenty of space, but if there is only just enough room, or you want to use the fewest suitcases you can get it all to fit in, then you may have a problem.

A *greedy algorithm* is a good alternative. It may not pack everything in as small a space as possible, but it will often do a good job. How do you choose what to try first? Be greedy. Put the biggest thing in and eat up as much space as you can. Then you place the next biggest, and so on. If you get to something that doesn't fit, then you put it in the next case. Intuitively, this works well because later when you have smaller spaces to fill, you will be trying to fill them with smaller objects. This is a good **heuristic**. Heuristics are just algorithms that do a good job, but not a perfect job. They do not guarantee to get the best answer.

Back on the road

The basic idea of a greedy algorithm applies to finding that salesman's tour. Applying the same **generalised** idea, at each step you just choose the town to visit next that is nearest to where you are now. That won't always get the best answer but it will usually get a good answer in a reasonable amount of time.

The good, the bad and the ugly

The same idea of finding tours round things that, if suitably **generalised**, are a graph, comes up over and over again in all sorts of problem areas. Once you've realised something is a graph, a whole host of algorithms then come for free. Some problems are then easy, while some turn out to be impossible. The most interesting ones though are those that quickly become impractical as the size of the problem grows. Getting the **representation** right matters, as does choosing the algorithm. It's important to recognise when a problem is so hard you are best going for a heuristic, for example.

Your choice of representation and algorithm can be good or bad. Some representations and algorithms are beautiful though, their elegance at solving a problem is just a delight.

Chapter 6

Bot Building for Human Beginners

Having seen the basics of computational thinking, let's explore how it might lead to building minds for robots. Building robot bodies is fun, but without a mind what can they do? We investigate the history of robot building, ask what understanding is all about, and then build a chatbot mind.

Robots have History

Give a robot a bad name?

The name *robot* was first used in a 1921 play R.U.R. (Rossum's Universal Robots) by the Czech political writer, *Karel Čapek*. In his play, an industrial plant on a secluded island is building humanoid work robots, who can 'work five times cheaper than humans'. As the play progresses, the familiar plot unfolds until by the end, would you believe it, all but one human has been killed by the robot revolution. And in a final act of self-sacrifice, he makes two robots fall in love and the curtain falls.

The play is widely seen to be a reflection of Čapek's concerns about a totalitarian society, explored through science fiction, thus the bleak storyline. If he had had a different politics to write about, it may have kick-started the media presence of robots on a less sinister tone. Stressing his point, the word robot, that Čapek chose, comes from the Czech word *robota* meaning 'serf labour'. Čapek had originally wanted to call the creatures *laboři* (from the Latin *labor*, to work), but decided against it, and asked his brother Josef for advice. Josef suggested *robota*. The Čapek family created both the motivation and name for robots in the west, just as the technology started to develop that would allow their actual construction.

What's a robot to you?

We all now have different ideas of what makes something a robot. A robot in its simplest terms, though, is a machine that's actions are guided by a program. We tend to think of robots as large mechanical men with world domination-related career paths, but the washing machine in the kitchen is actually also a robot. It is controlled by a computer and its less megalomaniac action is to wash clothes at various speeds and heats. Similarly, 'robots' can be made just of software. They can be programs that carry out actions in the digital world, like playing virtual characters in video games, scraping data from websites to create new knowledge or controlling virus-infected computers. These virtual robots are called *bots*, and although they lack a physical body, they do what robots are defined to do.

Let's first do a quick tour of the history of physical robots, but then look at the more interesting part: building their minds.

Tales of history and imagination

Tales of physical robots have actually been a staple of human history the world over. In third century ancient China, the Lie Zi text describes a humanoid robot built by mechanical engineer *Yan Shi* for the Chinese emperor, *King Mu of Zhou*. It was a life-size, human-shaped figure made of leather, wood, and artificial organs. The mythology of Ancient Crete includes Talos, a man of bronze guarding the island of Europa from pirates, and Jewish legend talks of clay golems, giant men of clay brought to life to follow written instructions placed in their mouths.

These all make interesting stories but in practical terms probably one of the first actual robot designers and builders was *Hero of Alexandria*, an Ancient Greek mathematician and inventor, who created moving machines powered by air pressure, steam and water. In the 13th century, the engineer *Al-Jazari* is thought to have described programmable humanoid automata in his 'Book of Knowledge of Ingenious Mechanical Devices' of 1206. This automaton was a boat with four musicians that floated on a lake to entertain guests. The music could be changed by changing the position of wooden pegs on a rotating drum so the pegs activated different percussion instruments at different times.

The creation of clockwork automata, exquisite mechanical dolls that performed entertaining tasks for the courts of Europe in the 18th century eventually evolved into electronic robots. Through the work of scientists such as *Walter Grey*, a pioneer of *cybernetics* (the study of how animals and machines control their behaviour), we started to see both the usefulness of robots, but also the complexity in building them.

Today there are robots other than washing machines in our homes. You may know someone with a vacuuming robot you can leave to clean the house while you are out, a robot that cuts the grass, or a car that can park itself. Modern aircraft have autopilots that now can even safely take off and land the plane on their own. If you've ever been on holiday when it was really foggy at the destination, the pilot may have handed over to the autopilot to land the plane. Why? Because it could do it more safely than the human. Similarly, self-driving cars are generally safer than human drivers. This is just the beginning of robots entering our lives, robots smart enough to learn how to do the job better than we can, by displaying ever more powerful *artificial intelligence* (AI).

Building Robot Minds

Build it in layers

The minds of robots are the really interesting part. So how do you build a mind? Different types of information are processed in different places in our brains but somehow are brought together to form a working whole. The same problem exists in robotics and AI.

It is fairly easy to create the simplest version of a robot mind: just an electronic circuit that makes a robot move around at random. The next step is to allow it to react to what is going on around it.

It is actually also easy to build simple machines that sense the world and react to what they sense in the way the simplest lifeforms do. For example, a simple robot might have a circuit that reverses a motor if it detects a loud sound. Another might stop when in a dark place. Yet another robot with a solar cell might move towards bright light allowing it to recharge (or 'feed'). Other robots might detect each other and aim to stay close as they move around.

Robots can, of course, have a different view of their world to us, based on different types of sensors. For example, we could build a robot that 'sees' using sonar, like a bat bouncing sounds off things around it and listening for the echoes. It could then change direction to avoid objects it detects in front of it.

If we take all of these components, each with a very simple way of reacting to the world, and blend them together, we start to get some interesting and more complex behaviours: robots that search out energy sources, but hide in a dark place at the first hint of danger, for example. Each component can be designed separately, then brought together to make a more complex whole. This is the computational thinking idea of **decomposition**, here applied to the design of robots, and yielding complex, animal-like behaviour.

Roboticist *Rodney Brooks* came up with a simple way to do this. His *subsumption architecture* is like a layer cake. Each layer, when active, causes a different behaviour, like wandering randomly, or reacting to light. Lower level behaviours are subsumed (included or absorbed) in higher layers when those higher layer behaviours are activated. This is a kind of **abstraction** combined with **decomposition**.

More complex robot control systems (higher layers) might have some simple internal representation of the world in them. They might know (using a **pattern matching** algorithm), for example, what sequence of behaviours to trigger and in what order when a particular situation, like hearing a danger signal, arises in the world the robot inhabits.

Occasionally, with an AI or robot system, rather than the behaviour being planned by the designer, the unexpected happens, and a series of simple behaviours triggered in the right order gives rise to *emergent behaviour*: patterns of behaviours happen that aren't in the individual behaviours that the robot is built with. For example, the software system, boids, mimics simple rules about how birds fly. It has rules such as moving in the same average direction of any nearby birds, while avoiding getting too close to your neighbours. From these simple rules, elegant replicas of the way real birds flock emerge.

Naturally selected

So far we have looked at directly engineering intelligent behaviour. There is another way: to create robot minds by a process similar to evolution by natural selection. The way natural selection works is based on the survival of the fittest. It's as though every generation of children are in a race to survive. Only if they do well in the race of life do they grow up and have children of their own (see Figure 41). Those who have children pass on features that led to their success to their own children, though with some mixing and mutation, meaning they aren't exact copies of their parents. They could be better or worse in the race of life. They must then compete themselves. As each generation passes, only those who do well in the race survive and gradually the population gets better at the race. In real life of course, this is going on continuously rather than in a series of rounds.

The **computational modelling** of this natural process has led to a new way of doing computation and of creating software. An initial population of possible designs are created, and each is tested with a *fitness test*, normally in a computer simulation. The individuals' solutions are ranked by their performance. The best performing ones are kept, but then changed at random in simple ways, including swapping features with other survivors, to make 'children' for the next generation. The other designs are discarded. This goes on over many thousands of generations inside the computer, testing and retesting designs, until the final champion emerges that is far better at the job than the originals it evolved from.

Learn to behave

Yet another way to build a mind is to create software that can learn. It's then shown lots and lots of examples of the desired behaviour

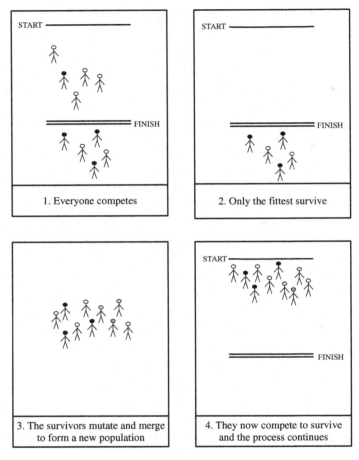

Figure 41: The process of evolution by natural selection as a race.

in different situations. Little by little it learns how to behave from the examples, teaching itself to behave the same way, by learning the patterns of behaviour. A variation of this is to let a machine learn by its mistakes. 'Punish' it when it gets things wrong, and 'reward' it when it gets things right. This time its software adjusts itself to repeat the good behaviour and avoid the bad, so that again it gradually behaves more and more in the way desired. We will explore this more in the next chapter.

How ever an AI is built, be it designed by human rule engineers, learnt its behaviour from lots of examples, or evolved through survival of the fittest, it will almost certainly use modular design, different components with different behaviours connected together to carry out a task: **decomposition**. This approach allows the modules to be tested individually and reused in other later systems, making the production of new robots both more robust and cheaper. It also means that ever more complex AIs can be built as individual components are improved, or new ones added, as we better understand each particular ability.

Build Your Own Chatbot

Let's talk about chatbots

Talking is one of the essences of humanity, so a good place to start to understand how computational thinking can be applied to AI is by visiting the psychotherapist. This particular psychotherapist was however a computer program called *ELIZA*, written at MIT by *Joseph Weizenbaum* in the mid-1960s. It was the first *chatbot*: a program designed to talk to people in a natural way. People would chat with ELIZA believing they were communicating with a real psychotherapist. As a bit of an in-joke Weizenbaum named ELIZA after Eliza Doolittle, a cockney flower-selling character from the play Pygmalion, who is taught to speak with an upper-class accent. This program was one of the first to successfully challenge the *Turing Test* for conversation: one of the most famous and influential tests for AI invented.

Am I human?

The premise of the Turing test is that if you can't tell the difference between AI and human skill, here chatting, the AI has passed the test and should be considered as intelligent as humans. It was suggested by mathematician and code-breaking computer scientist, *Alan Turing*, who supposedly got the idea from a Victorian Parlour game.

In the game, a man and a woman leave the room, and everyone else thinks up questions to ask them. The questions are written on cards and passed out to the man and woman. They write their answers and pass them back, where they are read out. The game is to work out who is the man and who the woman just from their answers. The twist is that the man is allowed to lie, but the woman must tell the truth (the Victorians presumably thought it wasn't right for women to lie, men on the other hand ...). If the man convinces people he is the woman, then he wins, otherwise the woman wins.

Turing realised you could do a similar thing with a machine. Instead of a man and a woman, he suggested putting a machine and a human in the other room, with the similar task of working out who was the machine just by asking questions. As with the man in the parlour game, the machine would do its best to deceive you. Turing argued that if you couldn't tell the difference after a long conversation, then you had to admit the machine was just as intelligent as the human.

As a way to pass the test, Weizenbaum chose to fake discussions with a psychotherapist for ELIZA, as this allowed some vagueness and changing of themes in the discussion, making it easier to fool people.

Modelling a chat

ELIZA was essentially a simple **computational model** of the way psychotherapists work, and more generally of how conversations between people work. First ELIZA had to use pattern matching to recognise specific words or phrases in the text typed in. It then used these cues to select from a list of pre-scripted output texts, or action rules, that are meaningful in the context. For example, if you mentioned your mother in the text you input, then ELIZA would detect this word and output a phrase like, "Tell me more about your early childhood". The chatbot designer, therefore, has the job of engineering ways to create a library of conditional rules IF x THEN y filling the x and y slots with suitable natural text relevant to the situation. The idea behind these rules is essentially the same as the ones we derived to solve logic puzzles, but here the problem to solve is to construct a believable conversation. Do it well and you create an illusion of understanding. ELIZA showed this was surprisingly easy to do, with simple code, particularly for short conversations. ELIZA's main computing steps are still found in many chatbots today.

It is debatable though that a machine that passes the Turing Test is really as intelligent as a human. Go back to the parlour game. Just because the man convinces everyone that he is the woman, doesn't mean he really is a woman, just that he is good at faking it. Similarly, if a machine passes a Turing test, perhaps it just means it is good at faking intelligence. By creating such models that are ever more convincing, though, we can test and improve our understanding of what and how human conversation works, and get a better idea of what we do and don't mean by intelligence.

Make up the mind of a chatbot

You can create your own chatbot, even without a computer. All you need are blank cards, a pen and a bit of thought. First decide what your chatbot will be designed for. This could be anything, but its an easy first step to focus on something you know well, perhaps your favourite sport or a TV show, as you know what makes a sensible conversation on these topics. Spend some time listening to real conversations and the kinds of things people say. Next you need a bit of **algorithmic thinking**. You need to come up with a set of cue words the chatbot will spot in the conversation, together with responses to it. You need an algorithm for your conversation. For example, suppose your chatbot is football mad (or soccer-mad if it is a US-chatbot) and 'free kick' (the cue) is mentioned by the other person. Your chatbot might respond with "Oh! Beckham's free kicks were amazing. Have you tried to bend it like Beckham?" You can probably come up with better ideas that will make a more natural conversation. Asking questions like ELIZA is a good idea as it makes the person do the real work. You will need to come up with lots of cues and responses to make it natural. It may be easier if you keep the subject narrow at least to start: one football team perhaps rather than anything about football. You also need some neutral things to say in case you don't match anything: remember part of **algorithmic**

thinking is having instructions for absolutely every eventuality! You don't want it to be repetitive though, so you need a wide range of neutral things to choose from.

On one set of cards write the cue words your chatbot will look for in the conversation. This is its input text. Give each cue card a number. Now clip these cue word cards together in alphabetical order. For example, your first few football-linked cards might be as in Figure 42, though you will need a lot more cues than this of course.

On a second set of cards, write the sentences that will be produced: the outputs. Label these with the number corresponding to the cue words that will trigger them. Clip the output text cards together too, but this time in numerical order. Figure 43 gives example response cards for the cues above.

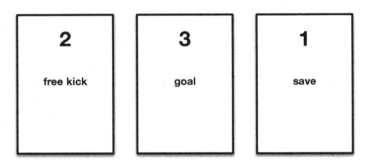

Figure 42: Sample cue cards for a football chatbot.

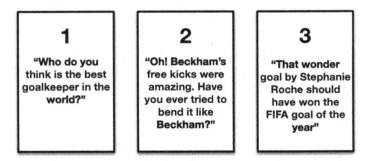

Figure 43: Sample response cards for the football chatbot.

Ordering the two sets of cards in this way will make your chatbot easier to operate. As the text comes in, you will be able to scan the words alphabetically, then immediately cross reference the numbers to get the right output card. You have just created an easy to use **representation** of your chatbot rules!

You need to **evaluate** your rules. So, once it's completed, give the sets of cards to a friend who will act as the computer running the chatbot program for you. Now have a chat. They should simply follow the instructions given by the cards. You have a normal conversation. Was your chatbot convincing? Would you have been fooled? Ask another friend to have a chat too and see what they think. Try doing it with someone by text without telling them they are talking to your chatbot!

Ask your friends, how good you chatbot was. Perhaps ask them to score it on a scale of 0–5. What were its strengths and weaknesses? What needs to be improved? What gave it away? That will point to answer cards that need to be changed or new ones that can be added. Answering these kinds of questions is another example of doing a *user evaluation* of your chatbot. As we saw computer scientists should always look to measure how successful their software is in doing what it was designed to do. **Evaluation** is an important part of computational thinking. Take the ideas from the user evaluation on board and refine your design and phrases. If you test again does it show an improved score? If not, why not? Once you have some experience of the kinds of chatbot conversations that work, if you can program, have a go at writing an actual chatbot program.

These days, rather than creating psychotherapists, chatbot designers try to fool us by doing things like pretending to be young non-English speakers to explain away the glitches, or they *crowd source* loads of real chat to extract patterns from them. Often chatbots are built, not by computer scientists, but by people who are good at creatively writing a believable character. They just use chatbot generation software: **generalised** chatbot programs that need the specific conversational aspects added. If you are good at creating believable characters, there is a career waiting for you populating virtual worlds with believable AI characters.

Beware of the bots?

Chatbots started off as an experiment in computing and psychology. They have expanded into an application that has lots of practical uses, such as characters to meet in all those virtual worlds, toys that want to be your friend, as a replacement for people in call centres, and even to be personal assistants, like Superhero Iron Man's AI butler, J.A.R.V.I.S.

However, along with its good side, chatbots have a dark side. They are faking people for lots of less than reputable reasons. The emergence of social media means that a chatbot's presence can be felt the world over. Experiments have showed that a set of chatbots deployed by researchers weren't detected as bots on social media sites, and actually ended up with thousands of followers. There are even cases where political activists have tried to use chatbots to sway public opinion, leading to a seemingly authentic swell of grass-root opinion that is actually generated by a crowd of opinionated bots. This so-called *astroturfing* could be used to try and affect views in, and so the results of, political elections. That undermines democracy. It is one example of the many areas where the legal and ethical issues round the legitimate uses of AI and robots are still unexplored. Online it is particularly important. We tend to think the web is populated by humans, but a survey in 2014 estimated that over 60% of internet traffic was generated by bots.

I wonder what ELIZA would make of that?

But does a Chatbot Understand?

Entering the Chinese room

IF-THEN *production rule* systems like our chatbot can be built to do complex things that mimic the way our brain operates in particular sets of circumstances. The real challenge of course is to build an AI or robot that can deal with everything a human can, rather than just pick the easy bits. People's ability to see, hear and sense the world with the speed and accuracy we do, communicate via written and spoken languages, fall in love, write a number one pop song, or make good decisions quickly when much of the information is unknown or vague, these are the abilities that allow us to survive in our complex world. We humans also have the ability to understand what we do, and that, for many, is a problem with AI. It follows rules, but it doesn't understand.

The philosopher, *John Searle* captured this problem in a thought experiment called *the Chinese room*. You are in a locked room with no knowledge of speaking or writing Chinese. You have a series of books that give you rules on how to translate Chinese. Messages from Chinese speakers outside the room are passed through a slot in the door. Inside the room, you look up the rules associated with the writing that arrives through the slot, follow them, and then slide the output back under the door. You are acting just like the chatbot following rules about what to 'say' in response to the messages that arrive. To those on the outside the answers to their questions, written in Chinese and pushed into the room, return sensibly answered in Chinese, so the room or something in the room must understand Chinese, mustn't it? But we know all that was happening was that you were following a complex set of rules to produce the output. You do not understand the questions or your answers. So does the room and its contents literally 'understand' Chinese? Or is it merely simulating the ability to understand Chinese? Searle calls the first position *strong AI* and the latter *weak AI*. Most people would say that the room doesn't understand anything. All the understanding resides with the people who came up with the rules. Many computer scientists and philosophers have argued over this thought experiment and the important questions it raises about understanding. Let's explore our own version of it.

The Klingon room

Very many people in the world have a basic knowledge of the Chinese language, which would prevent them from being locked away in this thought experiment. Chinese is also an intricate language used by millions, but evolved over the centuries and carrying its own peculiar turns of phrase and exceptions. It's a living natural language with massive scope and complexity. It would be really difficult to actually create the rules needed to make the room work. That undermines the experiment a bit. So let's think of something simpler that is more conceivably possible to build.

Do you speak Klingon? For the thought experiment, any language will do so long as someone understands it. Klingon, is a recent example of a language with its own vocabulary, grammar and alphabet created by *Marc Okrand*, in honour of the Star Trek science fiction universe. It makes a useful, simpler alternative to Chinese. It is a language with a *synthetic syntax*: grammatical rules for building the sentences that we have had complete oversight of from the beginning. We know exactly how the language was built, its rules and *syntax*, its *semantics* (what words and sentences mean) and how its verbs and nouns work. There are even some fluent human speakers of this extra-terrestrial language. Therefore, it is easier to see that creating the Klingon translation books in the room is a practical possibility. This is especially so, given we know the full scope of what the language can convey, which is mostly, and not unsurprisingly, about fighting, honour and spaceships. For example, the Klingon for 'bridge' as in a star ship, was well established early on. It was many years later that the concept of a bridge as a way to cross over water was assimilated into the language. It is rather an extreme artificial example of how *semantics*, the meaning of languages, evolve, how we come to a shared understanding of what words mean. In real human languages, this often happens over centuries, and the exact process is often hard to track.

It's clearly possible to create a Klingon room. So would such a room, containing someone who knew nothing about Klingon, understand Klingon if it answered questions in a similar way to the Chinese room?

A twist

Let's add a twist to create our own thought experiment. Let's have one Chinese room with Chinese questioners and one Klingon room with fandoms finest Klingon questioners outside the room. Would those outside the Chinese room feel their room had a lesser understanding of their language, because the translation books were just too difficult to create and so didn't quite get it right all the time: could all the complex nuances of a real living language be captured? Would our Klingon questioners, with their world view drenched in concepts of honour and combat, feel their room gave better quality replies as it has a smaller world to understand? If that was the case, then perhaps the argument is that the translation books' rules just need to have the meaning (the semantics), as well as the words and grammar (the syntax). It would suggest that if we could create enough exacting rules to cover the real world, then the rooms would actually understand?

What do you think?

Chapter 7

Build a Brain

Rather than trying to engineer a mind directly, we'll now use computational thinking to build a simple brain from the bottom up. It will help us explore how our brains, built of lots of nerve cells linked together, actually work, and how this leads to the complex behaviour of humans. We will then start to see how one might create an Artificial Intelligence that doesn't just do what we do, but does it because it has a brain that works the same way. Perhaps if we manage to accurately build a brain, a mind will just emerge.

Building a Learning Brain

Artificial intelligence goes to card school

We've seen that computers blindly follow instructions written for them: algorithms. That gives them power but its hard to claim they are intelligent. We show our intelligence not just in being able to solve specific problems, but in our ability to be flexible. We learn. They don't. Learning is a key part of being intelligent, so how could an artificial intelligence possibly learn, when it has to just follow the instructions given it? We need to create an algorithm for learning!

Let's start with a really simple task for an AI to learn, checking it has the right number of coins. Let's be more precise. What exactly do we want this simple AI to learn to do? Well, we want it to be able to tell us there are two coins present, but only when two coins are present. It shouldn't do anything if there are no coins, or if there is only one coin on the table. We will assume it has a mechanism for sensing coins, but it's going to have to learn to count them.

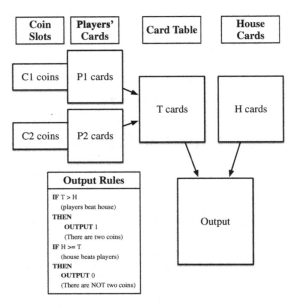

Figure 44: The board for our learning brain.

To explain this way of learning, we will use a simple board-game version of a *learning machine*. It uses the board shown in Figure 44, together with a set of cards (it doesn't matter what is on them). By playing a series of rounds of the game, the machine will learn to correctly check it has the right number of coins. Players place a coin (or not) and this will lead to cards moving around the table, being added, and the numbers compared. Ultimately, the machine will output its answer.

The machine has two slots, where the two players each place their coin to be counted. The cards held by each player are put on their positions on the board. There is also a card table area where the cards are played, and an area for the house's cards to be placed. The result card for the round is placed in the final, output, area of the board. There are two result cards to choose from, one marked 0 and the other marked 1.

The card game runs left-to-right like this. We start by dealing a small, random number of cards to the two players and to the house: P1, P2 and H cards, respectively. We then play a series of rounds.

Each player has to put a coin in the slot to be allowed to play in a given round. This releases their corresponding hand of P1 or P2 cards. They go onto the card table area (which will add together to be T cards altogether). That total goes up against the house cards' hand. If there are more player cards in total, T, than the house hand of H cards (T > H), then the players have won. In that situation, the output is a 1. We want that eventually to mean: "There are two coins". If the house wins, 0 is output, which we hope will mean "There are NOT two coins". In either case, the players' hands go back to where they started for the next round.

As the number of cards dealt is random, and that number determines what it does, the board-game brain will act randomly. By repeatedly playing the game, we want our brain to learn, changing the initial random numbers of cards to ones that always triumph the way we want. That is, by the end it should output 1 only when there are two coins present. The result we are after is summarised in Figure 45.

The machine learns to do this by playing a series of rounds, and after each round we apply the following simple *production rules* where C1 stands for the number of coins placed by Player 1 (one coin or none) and C2 stands for the number of coins placed by Player 2.

Rule R1:

> **IF** the game played gives the correct output,
> **THEN** do nothing: don't change the number of cards.

C1	C2	Output
0	0	0
0	1	0
1	0	0
1	1	1

Figure 45: The outputs we want our board-game brain to learn.

Rule R2:

IF the game played gives an output of 1, but we wanted an output of 0 to match the output table,

THEN remove C1 cards from Player 1 and remove C2 cards from Player 2.

Rule R3:

IF the game played gives an output of 0 but we wanted an output 1,

THEN add C1 cards to Player 1 and add C2 cards to Player 2.

These rules are our brain's algorithm for learning. Time to **evaluate** them, so let's look at some examples.

Example Game 1: lucky deal, all's well!

Suppose, the numbers of cards currently in play on the board are three cards dealt to Player 1, four cards dealt to Player 2 and five cards dealt to the house ($P1 = 3, P2 = 4, H = 5$). There is a coin in slot 1 (C1 is 1) but no coin in slot 2 (C2 is 0). We will write that $(C1, C2) = (1, 0)$.

As there is a coin in slot 1 (C1 is 1), the three P1 cards go forward on to the table, but the P2 cards don't as C2 is 0, so on the card table we have three cards (see Figure 46).

We can **generalise** the number of cards, T, that go on the table. It can always be calculated using the equation:

$$T = ((C1 \times P1) + (C2 \times P2)).$$

In our example, it gives $(1 \times 3 + 0 \times 4) = (3 + 0) = 3$. Notice how the multiplications mean that C1 and C2's values determine whether the corresponding values are added in. A 0 makes the P value disappear from the sum. A 1 keeps it there.

So the sum, T, is 3 for our brain and that is less than H which is 5, $(3 < 5)$ so the card marked 0 is placed on the Output of the brain: "There are NOT two coins". This is the output we want when only one coin has been played, so we apply Rule R1 and do nothing.

We try the next selection. All the cards go back to where they came from. This time, let's put a coin in both slots, though, so

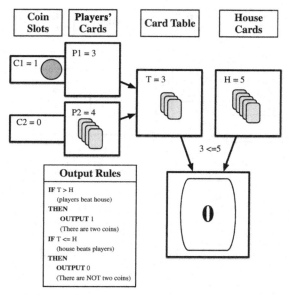

Figure 46: An example round for our learning brain. As there is only a coin in slot 1 only the first player's cards are moved from their hand to the table area. There are less cards, T, on the table than house cards so the output is 0.

$(C1, C2) = (1, 1)$. Both players' cards now go forward to the table as there are coins in both slots, leaving six cards there: $(1 \times 3 + 1 \times 4) = 7$. Now, $7 > 5$ so the output of the brain is 1 as we want: "There are two coins". We do nothing, following Rule R1 again.

In fact, if we try all the four combinations of coins in the slots, each one of them gives us the correct output. Yippee! No learning needed. We were lucky there, though. Our initial cards dealt, of three, four and five, just happened to give us cards in the hands that made the machine work fine. With those card numbers, it can always correctly tell us whether there are two coins present or not. But what happens if we are not so lucky? Our game will then need to change its ways, and learn how to behave. Let's see with another game.

Example Game 2: the game needs playing

We start by dealing our smallish random hands again. On the table this time Player 1 has six cards, Player 2 has four cards, and the house has four cards.

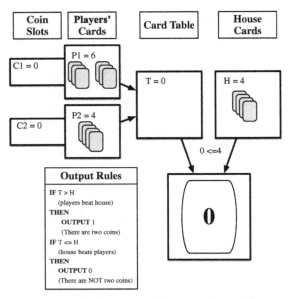

Figure 47: A new learning brain game. There are no coins, so no cards go on to the table area. There are less cards, T, on the table than house cards so the output is 0.

The situation with no coins in the slots where both C1 and C2 are 0 is easy. No cards move, and for the house hand, $0 < 4$ so the output is 0: "There are NOT two coins". The condition $(C1, C2) = (0, 0)$ is correct. This is shown in Figure 47.

With a coin only in slot 2 so $(C1, C2) = (0, 1)$, Player 2's hand moves forward. Player 1's stays fixed, and four cards go on the table $(C2 \times P2 = 4)$, but that's not enough to win. The house also has four cards. The output is 0: "There are NOT two coins". Remember the cards on the table need to total more than (not just equal to) H to make the output 1, so no change, following Rule R1 yet again. The condition $(C1, C2) = (0, 1)$ is correct.

Now pop a coin in slot, C1, and none in C2. Again, we want this to output 0, but follow the cards! On the card table we have $6 \geq 4$, so the output is a 1, and that's wrong! We must apply Rule R2. It said:

"**IF** the game played gives an output of 1, but we wanted an output of 0 to match the output table,

THEN we remove C1 cards from Player 1 and remove C2 cards from Player 2."

This means that, since C1 is 1 and C2 is 0, we remove a card from Player 1 but none from Player 2. The new value of P1 is 5 ($6 - 1$) and P2 remains as 4.

Having taken away a card from Player 1's pile, we move the hand back. We have taken nothing from Player 2's cards. The machine has started to learn.

We now select another condition and try again. As you experiment with this example you will come back to $(C1, C2) = (1, 0)$ as you cycle through the possible inputs, and again there will be an error. Again, Rule R2 will be applied, and the machine will learn a little more. This time when the card is removed from P1, it becomes 4.

At this point, P1 = 4, P2 = 4, H = 4. Now when that same situation comes round again, it will actually work as there are four player cards played and four house cards played. The output for $(C1, C2) = (1, 0)$ will be 0: "There are NOT two coins", which is what we want. You will find the case of $(C1, C2) = (1, 1)$ works correctly too. For that condition, the final reduced value of $P1(4) + P2(4)$ is 8. The house value is 4 and $8 > 4$.

The game machine has learnt to act in the right way, just by being played, and adjusting its cards when it got things wrong. The rules of the game are an algorithm for learning.

Let's not worry about being negative

Experiment with the game yourself. You will find that you need to apply all the rules, R1–R3, at some point depending on the cards dealt at the start of the game, but doing so will help the game to learn the right behaviour. It depends on where you start and the order you chose to put the coins in the slots (the various conditions), but eventually you will get there. If the game's rules require you to take away more cards than you have in a hand, you go over to the good old fashioned IOU. Write a note saying −1 card or −2 cards, and continue to play, checking you get the right answer for each of the conditions you want. At the end, you will have card hands P1 and P2 which will either contain cards or perhaps an IOU, but the game will still have learned.

What's in a brainy game?

What you have actually been doing in this game is to create a learning module for a brain to calculate the logic function AND. It learns to tell you if there is a coin in slot 1 AND a coin in slot 2. We didn't program the logic of AND though, the module learnt to calculate it. The way the board game learns is based on an idea called a *neural network*.

A neural network mimics (i.e., models) the way the brain does computing at a very basic level: it is an **abstraction**. All those billions of nerve cells, called *neurons*, in your brain can be thought of as simple processing devices. They connect to other neurons through specialist nerve elements called *axons*, and collect signals from other parts of the neural circuit. Then if the signal coming into the part of the cell called the *synapse* is high enough (higher than the weight threshold of that neuron), it fires a signal out to other neurons that it is connected to.

Our board-game models a single neuron. The inputs for the neuron are played by the coins. We want a circuit that fires (output 1), only when two signals are present (like having two coins in the slots). The cards in the hand represent the neural weights. They are the changing parts of the neuron that helps it to learn. The number of cards given to the house is acting like the threshold of the neuron. At the start, neurons don't know how to add together the signals coming in. To start with, they fire randomly, just like the random cards we dealt. The weights are potentially all over the place. After all, how can a single building block neuron know what the brain as a whole is trying to do? They need to learn, and they do that in the same way as the card game. They get a signal saying whether their output is right or wrong (that's why we call it *supervised learning*) and change their internal weights accordingly, strengthening some connections and weakening others using learning rules similar to the *production rules*, R1, R2 and R3 that we used. These interconnection weights can be positive (like the cards in the hands) or negative (like the IOUs), representing a negative weight.

The game creates a **computational model** of how neurons work. We have provided an algorithmic version of neurons, that when simulated does seem to do the right thing. It learns. We did it using a physical game, but we could implement it all in software. Then we could create models with thousands, maybe millions of neurons. That would allow us to explore if our understanding of how neurons behave, really is correct. Does it start to behave like a simple brain?

Boolean for you

So that's the biological learning bit done, what about the AND logic function mentioned? AND is an example of a *Boolean operator*. You can think of Boolean operators as tables (like Figure 45) that work with *Boolean* values: TRUE (1) and FALSE (0). They provide the foundation of logic. They were devised by 19th-century mathematician, *George Boole*, a fascinating character, who, with his maths abilities, started his own school in Lincoln at the age of 19. He had a successful career but died unexpectedly at the age of 49. The story goes he had walked over two miles in the drenching rain and decided to lecture wearing his soggy clothes. Not surprisingly he developed a severe fever. Ill-advisedly his wife Mary, who was a recent convert to homoeopathy, decided the best way to treat him was to use a remedy that 'resembled the source'. So she poured buckets of water over him in bed. Needless to say his condition worsened and he died on December 8, 1864.

Boole's work laid the foundation for ideas in digital electronic circuits we still use today in the form of digital *logic gates*. Millions are etched into the silicon of a single microprocessor making it able to compute complex sums rapidly. What is actually etched on to the silicon are *transistors*, but it is hard to work out how to design things in terms of just transistors. Instead, transistors are grouped into logic gates. Having designed the *AND gate* (fire if both inputs present), an *OR gate* (fire if at least one input is present), and so on, the designer thinks about them and forgets about the transistors underneath. The detail of the transistors can be ignored. This provides a first level of **abstraction** in the design of digital electronics. Logic gates themselves are grouped into components that do more complicated things like adding and multiplying, or moving data from here to there, and those functions provide an even higher level of **abstraction**. The designer then no longer needs to think about the logic gates but can think in terms of these more sophisticated functions instead. In fact, circuit designers make use of lots of layers of **abstraction**, going ever higher as the chips they design get more and more complicated. Looked at in a different way this is an example of **decomposition**. To build a calculating unit, we make it out of adder units, multipliers, and so on. But how do we build an adder? Design that in terms of logic gates. Logic gates? Design them out of transistors. Modern microprocessor chips are more complex than the road network of the whole planet Earth. Designing them is only possible using computational thinking on a massive scale.

Logic gates don't have to be created out of transistors. They can also be created, as we have seen, out of simple neural circuits too. You could substitute the transistor-based logic gates with equivalent neural based ones, and it would work the same. Researchers in computer science and electronics labs around the world are looking at ways to take the power of biological brain-inspired computing, including looking at how the pulses in brain circuits change over time, and how to build them into fast-learning silicon or germanium microchips. **Algorithmic thinking** works both ways. It not only gives us a new way to do science, but creating algorithmic versions of the way the world works can sometimes give us whole new ways to make computers work.

Our simple coin counting circuit that learns from scratch to adapt to do its job correctly is doing something trivially simple, but when it joins with millions of other similar learning circuits, and they all pull together they have the potential to create a massive computational army. Of course the real trick is how to program them, how to develop the software, to let them work together to a common goal.

Neural Snap!

Snap! Not as easy as it looks

Our coin checking game wasn't much of a game. How about learning an actual game-like Snap! If two cards match, shout "SNAP!" If they are different stay quiet. To keep it simple, we will assume we only have red and black cards. Can we create a neural network to play the game?

Let's spell out exactly what we need it to do to detect a colour match. Let's represent red by 1 and black by 0. Red–Red (1,1) or Black–Black (0,0) is snap, Red–Black (1,0) or Black–Red (0,1) isn't. This is a lot like the logic of our AND coin checker, but it is not as simple as that to learn.

Colour snap is an example of a logical *exclusive-or* (XOR) function. It is a bit like an OR function but instead an XOR only fires with inputs (1,0) and (0,1) and not with any other inputs. The exclusive part is that it fires exclusively if one input is true (i.e., is 1), but not if both are true, as in Figure 48.

Back in the early days of neural networks, this sort of logic became a big problem. The neural circuits, back then called *perceptrons*, were great at AND, OR and other similar Boolean logic functions, but they couldn't deal with that pesky exclusive part. The reason was their geometry. It was realised that a perceptron worked because it created a decision boundary, a line on a graph. With enough input, the perceptron was pushed over the boundary. That was dependant on the weights and thresholds in the circuit (our P1, P2 and H values from earlier). So as long as the things you wanted to give separate outputs for were on opposite sides of the single decision boundary line all was fine, the perceptron worked.

Input Colours	Input Coordinates	Output	Shout Snap or keep quiet?
(Black, Black)	(0,0)	0	"SNAP!"
(Black, Red)	(0,1)	1	
(Red, Black)	(1,0)	1	
(Red, Red)	(1,1)	0	"SNAP!"

Figure 48: The outputs needed for a snap-playing neural network.

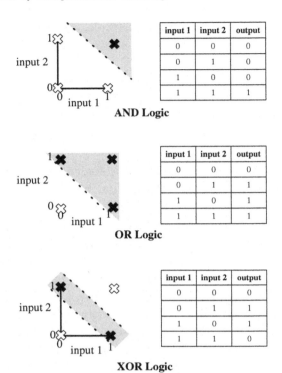

input 1	input 2	output
0	0	0
0	1	0
1	0	0
1	1	1

AND Logic

input 1	input 2	output
0	0	0
0	1	1
1	0	1
1	1	1

OR Logic

input 1	input 2	output
0	0	0
0	1	1
1	0	1
1	1	0

XOR Logic

Figure 49: Graphs of AND, OR and XOR. An output 0 for a given pair of inputs is marked with a white cross. An output 1 is marked with a black cross. AND and OR have straight decision boundaries: a single line can be drawn to divide the white and black cross. For XOR, no such straight line can be drawn. It needs two lines.

But in the case of an XOR function where we want the line as in the table in Figure 48 things didn't work. If we draw these on a graph using the coordinates given (where a red is 1 and a black is 0), there is no possible single straight line that separates the output 0 answers from the output 1 answers. You can't create a system where pushing you over a line flips from one state to the other. See Figure 49.

Then an idea: if each perceptron can only draw a single line, use more perceptrons. If we have one perceptron feeding into a second perceptron, a so-called *multi-layer perceptron*, then each layer can define a decision line and we will have two lines to play with.

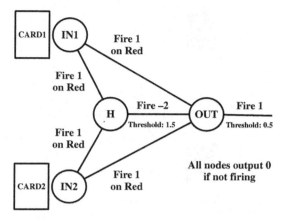

Figure 50: A neural network to play snap. Circles are neurons. Each node has a threshold the signal coming in must beat before that neuron fires. The number on the edge gives the strength of signal when it does fire. When not firing each neuron outputs 0.

Can we build it?

Can we build it? Yes, we can. There are several ways to build neural circuits that do exclusive-or, so could play Snap, and Figure 50 gives one. Notice we are using a *graph* **representation** here to describe brain circuitry: it is after all about places and links between them (neurons and their connections). We are also now **abstracting** away from the internal details of how the neurons work, focussing on their learnt behaviour.

Our neural network is now built of four neurons connected together. We have two input neurons, IN1 and IN2, that detect the colour of the cards they are shown. They will output a 1 if the card is red and 0 if it's black. That output goes to a neuron, H, in a second layer. It has a threshold to fire of 1.5, (i.e., it will only fire if the inputs add to more than 1.5), but its output is negative (-2) when it fires. All the signals go to a third neuron, OUT, with a threshold of 0.5.

We need to test it. Let's go through all the combinations.

(Black, Black) cards in gives 0 out

If $(0, 0)$ goes in, that's (Black, Black), the neuron in the second layer, H, gets a 0 input from both connections (see Figure 51(a)). At H, 0 is

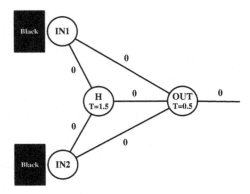

(a) The Snap Neural network on seeing (Black, Black).

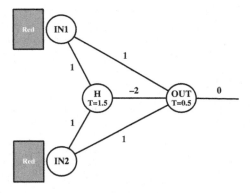

(b) The Snap Neural network on seeing (Red, Red).

Figure 51: The Snap Neural network on seeing cards of the same colour.

less than the threshold 1.5 so node H fires a 0. The signals arriving at the OUT neuron are added $(0 + 0 + 0)$ giving 0 at H's output. This is less than the 0.5 threshold of the OUT neuron, so it doesn't fire and the perceptron as a whole gives output 0.

(Red, Red) cards in gives 0 out

With $(1, 1)$ going in (Red, Red), H receives $(1+1)$ which is 2. That is more than 1.5, so H fires, outputting -2. At OUT, we have the signals direct from the input layers, 1 and 1, which add to the weighted signal

Build a Brain 111

-2 from H, to give $(1 + 1 + (-2))$ which is 0. This is less than the threshold of OUT, so the output is 0 (see Figure 51(b)).

(Black, Red) cards in gives 1 out

If $(0,1)$ goes in, that's (Black, Red), then H only gets a 1 which is less than it's threshold, so H doesn't fire. At OUT, we get a 0 from IN1 due to the Black at the input, a 1 from IN2 from the Red at the other input. They combine with the 0 from H, to give $(0 + 1 + 0)$ which sums to 1. That is greater than 0.5 so the output fires giving 1 from OUT (see Figure 52(a)).

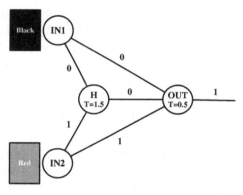

(a) The Snap Neural network on seeing (Black, Red).

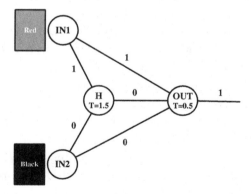

(b) The Snap Neural network on seeing (Red, Black).

Figure 52: The snap neural network on seeing cards of different colours.

(Red, Black) cards in gives 1 out

Work through the last case of input (1, 0) so (Red, Black) yourself and you will find that the output from OUT is a 1 as in Figure 52(b).

Overall, this pattern of inputs and outputs matches the XOR table. It is just what we need to play our game correctly. We have built the bits of brain that can play colour snap.

A qualia and a cup of blue coffee please

In the last chapter, we looked at whether chatbots understand. We've now seen that we can create brains from artificial neurons. Let's think about neurons and look at understanding from a different angle. Humans understand, they are conscious, and they experience *qualia*. Qualia is a term related to our internal experiences and perception. Take, for example, the taste of coffee, or the blueness of a clear sky. We all know what they are like, but how can you explain them to someone else? What is coffeeness or blueness? If we accept that the brain causes the mind (there are researchers who don't), then something about the way the neurons and structures in the brain act, gives rise to these behaviours as well as simple actions, the emergence of meaning, our qualia, and even our emotions like love. If we can accurately model the parts of the brain that matter to create all these internal experiences, then arguably our artificial brain should also experience them all, including qualia. It is all about getting the right **abstraction**, modelling the features of the brain that matter to generate these experiences, while only leaving out those that don't. However, finding and isolating these parts is a massive challenge for neuroscientists and computer scientists.

We are coming to realise that the active work in our brains isn't just done by the neurons, though. There are other cells in the brain that seem to process information too, and other chemical transmitters wash through our brains affecting their operation. Different types of information are selected to be processed in different places in the brain, yet somehow this all joins together to give us... well, us and our understanding of our world. But if we look at a single neuron in say the *amygdala*, that part of the brain that seems to generate emotions, it is simply firing or not firing depending on the amount of electrochemical signal coming into it. It has no understanding that in the larger picture it is helping to generate a feeling of fear in the individual. It's just a switch, and it's just switching.

Even with the new techniques of so-called *deep learning*, where the massive increase in computer power available and new mathematical algorithms allows multiple layers of neurons to be programmed to learn to perform useful tasks like medical drug discovery, tagging pictures with a written description or predicting the weather or the stockmarket we still don't understand how the brain generates many of our human characteristics. There are other researchers who are interested in how patterns of activity in the brain change over time. They have built clever electronic circuits called *spiking neurons*, that send out sequences of electronic pulses, mimicking the way that brain neurons fire then relax then fire again. They hope that understanding the temporal, time-dependant properties, of these systems will bring us new understanding and allow us to build new applications. It's clear that getting the right **abstraction** for understanding the brain is critical and though there has been significant advances in this area, it's still an exciting exploration of the Unknown.

The study of real brains and behaviours and comparing those with computer intelligence is still an area with deep philosophical questions to be answered. Having artificially intelligent computers, however, gives us machines that we can use to explore these deep questions, questions that cut right to the core of what it means to be human, while on the way, creating useful tools and applications to help us in our lives. You will have your own opinions and thoughts on these questions, and quite right too. You are only human after all.

Chapter 8

Building a Scam Bot

Having seen the basics of brain and chatbot building, and how some chatbots have been turned to the Dark Side of computing, let's now put it all together. It's time to explore how we might build a simple bot brain that can con humans. As a result, we will see why computational thinkers, whether human or machine, need ethical thinking too. Robots first entered the scene with world domination on their minds, so we will also explore some reasons why robots may never manage to rule the world.

A Fortune-Telling Mind

A machine with mysteries incorporated

After our brief journey into the mysteries of the human mind, it seems appropriate to build a mysterious, mischievous artificial intelligence (AI) so we can explore other ideas in robotics and AI.

We are now going to build an AI version of a fake fortune teller, for educational purposes only of course, to give us a chance to look at the computational thinking behind the scenes. This scam is created by a number of cunning components blended together. Let's see how. We will need an underlying scam, a way to pull people into it, a way to check the punter has handed over the money, and a way to check if two cards turned over are the same colour. Let look at each in turn.

Fortune favours the brave

Imagine the scene... The room is dim and filled with exotic scents. Through the gloom can be glimpsed strange symbols and unusual manuscripts in long forgotten lore. Crystals sit upon the table, shattered shards from mysterious times, long forgotten. Almost imperceptibly the fortune teller, an AI, enters and bids you to sit. The session begins.

> *"Welcome. The crystals indicate your vibrations are receptive today. I sense a pull of destiny. Your aura marks you as positive and cheerful, but there has been a time in the past when you were upset, when perhaps you were too critical of yourself. You know you have hidden abilities that you have been as yet unable to use to help yourself and others in the way you want. You understand for progress to occur, the need to bring harmony with others, while remaining true to yourself."*
>
> *"I can help. I can, for the cost of just two coins, ascertain the unique card in a pack that will help symbolise and signpost the future path you must follow to bring harmony and good luck wherever you carry it."*
>
> *"I sense you have doubts, I must prove the synergy, the power of a linkage is correct. To test this here, you must choose a card using your free will, if the colours of the two cards, your choice and mine, match, as I predict they must, it is proof of the link. Should I fail, I will pay a forfeit and give you three coins back: an additional coin to account for the grievous error in my predication."*
>
> *"Are you ready to discover your future in the cards? You clearly have nothing to lose and everything to gain!"*

The session ends... Twice

Ending one: You pay the two coins, the fortune teller chooses your lucky card, then you choose a card totally at random from the pack. The colours match, both are red. You have your lucky card, and your proof that it summons a similar coloured card. The link is there. Having then had your fortune told based on the cards, you leave the room as the fortune teller, clearly exhausted from pulling together the cosmic threads, pockets the coins and quietly leaves the room.

Ending two: You pay the two coins, your lucky card is revealed, you choose a second card, sadly the colours differ: red and black.

The promised proof of a psychic link is not there. The fortune teller apologises: the auric plane was misaligned today, and you are given the three coins promised, your original two and an extra coin for the disappointment. The fortune teller apologises again. Perhaps the next time, but you have gained rather than lost. You leave the room materially richer than you entered, but perhaps wondering if you will return another day when the omens are better?

Whatever ending occurs, the whole thing is a money making scam, but how can it work? It seems so fair, and why are people taken in by such scams in reality?

The scam

How does the scam play. Let's see how the mystery of the maths turns seemingly fair to fundamentally foul. At the centre of this is a simple mathematical mistake that people are tempted into here by the flim-flam of the fortune teller's personality and script (more on that later). Looking at the maths, if our AI fortune teller gets the lucky cards to match correctly, then it makes two coins profit. If the fortune teller gets the card match wrong, it pays three coins. That seems quite a penalty until you remember that two of these coins are the ones you already gave the fortune telling, AI. So it only loses one extra coin from its money bank if the cards don't match.

Wisdom suggests we look at the probabilities here. The lucky card, nonsense as it is, is just any card chosen from a full deck. The test card, well that's another random card pulled from the remaining deck. So it's like playing a game of colour snap from a full shuffled deck. There is as much of a chance of the two cards matching in colour, black and black, or red and red, as there is of the cards not matching in colour, red and black or black and red. It's a 50:50 chance.

If our AI fake fortune teller plays a sequence of these scams, the money starts to mount up. Why? Suppose 10 victims fall for the scam. On average, doing this 10 times, 50% (five) of them, will win the money back because the cards won't match, but 50%, five of them, will leave and take no cash with them. Figure 53 summarises the situation.

On average from 10 victims	Profit Calculation	Explanation	Final Profit / Loss
5 colour matches	5 × 2 coins profit	2 coins profit per colour match	10 coins profit
5 colour non-matches	5 × 1 coin loss	2 of the 3 coins returned per non-match were the victims	5 coin loss
		Therefore, overall average profit to AI	5 coin profit

Figure 53: Alternatives and profits of running the scam 10 times.

The more people who play the scam the more money the AI con artist can make. This is an error we make quite easily. It is about not actually seeing the long term, real mathematical consequences of things we do. It happens a lot, and not just in unethical acts like this one. For example, the birthday paradox tells us that, unexpectedly, it takes just 23 people in a room for there to be a 50% chance that two people there share a birthday.

Get em in by building a Barnum

We know the scam now, but how do we persuade people to take part? The underlying scam mathematics sound convincing if you don't think about it too much, you have nothing to lose, it seems, so have everything to play for. But there are other ways we can convince people to take part. We have looked at *chatbots* already in Chapter 6, AI systems that can mimic conversations. That is useful for general discussions, but can we create a chatbot front end that seems convincing as a fortune teller?

It must seem to be able to predict things about us as soon as we sit down. It does this even before it offers to find our lucky card. How does a fake chatbot fortune teller gain our confidence? The answer is it uses what are called *Barnum statements*, to build the trust by manipulating our perception of language. They are named after the famous circus promoter, *Phineas T. Barnum* who was notorious for promoting hoaxes. The Barnum effect is based on the fact that people will tend to believe that a description of them is accurate when in fact the statements are actually applicable to large numbers of people: statements like "at times you have doubts as to whether you chose the right thing to do", or "some of your dreams tend to be pretty unrealistic". Doh! They of course apply to everyone, but were rated by people in experiments as applying specifically to them. Our AI fortune teller's dialogue at the start is built using Barnum statements. That means that even though it's just using generalisations, the way we process the meaning will tend to make us believe that the AI knows something deep and mystical about us. It therefore pulls us into the lucky card scam.

Like any chatbot you could include a more complex dialogue. It doesn't have to follow exactly the same script. It could have a large collection of Barnum statements to choose from. The choice could be random but more convincingly, perhaps, it could tailor what it says as part of an initial conversation, where the replies from its victim trigger different, and perhaps more appropriate, Barnum statements. The complexity would be up to you as the designer.

Building it bit by bit

So we now have a convincing scam to use, and a chatbot to draw in the punters and make them part with their money. If we are to build an AI to pull off the whole scam it needs two more elements. It needs to be able to check the punter really has parted with the money, as otherwise it might find it is the one being conned if it has been happily giving out money but not taking any in! It needs to be able to check the victim has put their two coins on the table. But we already built that — we just need one of our trained up *neural networks* from Chapter 7.

We also need it to be able to tell when it can take the money and when it must pay up. It needs to be able to check whether the two chosen cards are the same colour. We've already built that too! We just need our other 'colour snap' playing neural network from Chapter 7.

We can build our spambot from a mixture of old and modified components: a general chatbot adapted to work with Barnum statements, our coin counter trained to behave the way we want it to and our snap-playing system adapted to check the cards and pay up or not rather than shout Snap!

We've just been playing the **decomposition** game again. Each part was built for its own purpose but with a bit of **generalisation** the separate modules can be brought together to make something new.

Ethics and World Domination

Designing and AI the right and wrong

This example has shown how various components, the Barnum chatbot front end, the coin counter and the colour snap player can be combined to create a working AI system. Each part can actually be built out of things found around the house: cards, paper and pens and coins. An AI doesn't need to be built on a computer, computation can be done in lots of different ways. Of course you could code up all the various components, the abstractions and algorithms, as a program to run on a computer too. But would it be a good thing to fill the world with such deceptive AI systems?

We have used it as a way of explaining computational elements like pattern matching, language processing, neural systems, and IF-THEN production rules, but computer scientists building real systems also need to consider the ethical issues in their work. What benefit will their systems give and to who? Are there some types of AI we should not design, and why? How far is it acceptable to manipulate humans' using these systems? For example, should we be building systems that mimic other humans with a wish to deceive, or to build dependency, or cause harm in some way? These issues are considered in the field of *ethics*, looking at what's morally right or wrong. Computer scientists are also subject to the law, but sometimes things can fall within the law and still cause harm. Is this AI fortune teller one such system? What do you and your friends think? Computing needs to live properly in the society around us, and future AI designers need to consider this.

The big question ... will Robots rule the world?

Ever since, the 1921 play, R.U.R, we started with several chapters ago that introduced the term 'robot', there has always seemed to be a latest film or show about robots or AIs trying to take over the world. But what relation do the evil AIs of the movies have to scientific reality? Could an AI take over the world? How would it do it? And why would it want to? AI movie villain writers need to consider the whodunit staples of motive and opportunity.

Finding a meaningful motive

Let's look at the motive. Few would say intelligence in itself unswervingly leads to a desire to rule the world. If you pass your school exams, is that an automatic cue for villainy? Of course not. In movies, AIs are often driven by self-preservation, a realisation that fearful humans might shut them down. But would we give our AI tools cause to feel threatened? They provide benefits for us and there also seems little reason in creating a sense of self-awareness in a system that just searches the web for the nearest Italian restaurant, for example.

Another popular motive for AIs' evilness is their zealous application of logic. For example, one theme is that the goal of protecting the earth can only be accomplished by wiping out humanity. This destruction by logic is reminiscent of the notion that a computer would select a stopped clock over one that is 2 seconds slow, as the stopped clock is right twice a day, whereas the slow one is never right. Such plot motivation, based on brittle logic combined with indifference to life, seems at odds with today's AI systems that reason mathematically with uncertainty and are built to work safely with people. One of the classic, science fiction writers, *Isaac Asimov*, thought this through in his robot collection 'I, Robot', where all robots had a built-in, un-tamperable rule set, the "Three laws of robotics", to prevent them harming humans.

Opportunity Knocks

When we consider an AI's opportunity to rule the world, we are on somewhat firmer ground. The famous *Turing Test* of machine intelligence was set up to measure a particular skill: the ability to conduct a believable conversation. The premise was that if you can't tell the difference between AI and human skill, the AI has passed the test and should be considered as intelligent as humans.

So what would a Turing Test for the 'skill' of world domination look like? To explore that we need to compare the antisocial AI behaviours with the attributes expected of human world domination. World dominators need to control important parts of our lives, say our access to money, or our ability to buy a house. AIs do that already: lending decisions are frequently made by an AI sifting through mountains of information to decide your credit worthiness, for example. AIs now trade on the stock market too.

An overlord would give orders and expect them to be followed. Anyone who has stood helplessly at a shop's self-service till as it makes repeated bagging related demands of them already knows what it feels like to be bossed about by AIs.

World domination bingo

Let's play world domination bingo to see how close AIs are to having the opportunity. You need to make up your own world domination bingo card. On a sheet of card draw a grid, say 3 by 3, and in each square write something you think makes for world domination. To help you come up with ideas, think about your favourite super villain ruling the world. What would they be doing that would let you know they were in charge? Controlling the Internet perhaps? Deciding where people can and can't go? Charging taxes even? Write one of the dastardly actions in each square on your bingo card until you have filled them all. Swap cards with a friend.

The rules are simple, each of you has to work against the clock doing a web search to find, and tick off, examples of computers, machines, robots or AI systems actually doing the activities on your card. You need to find as many as you can. When you find an example, make a note of the webpage and score the activity out on the grid. Try and find a set of different activities that make a straight line, horizontally or vertically, just like in normal Bingo.

The first person to get a line shouts Bingo (in an evil robot voice of course) and wins, but check the examples ticked off and the activities detailed on the webpages match. If you only have a fixed amount of time to play, the winner is the person with the most squares ticked, but again check the card to be sure the examples you have found are real and match the super villain activity in the bingo card squares.

Playing this game will give you a better idea of what today's robots and AIs can really do, after which you can either start to worry or feel safer.

Kill Bill?

No megalomaniac Hollywood robot would be complete without at least some desire to kill us. We already have drones that are designed to kill. Military robots can identify targets without human intervention. It is currently a human controller that gives permission to attack but it's not a stretch to say that the potential to auto-kill exists in these AIs. We would need to change the computer code to allow it, though. Autonomous killing robots do already exist, in fact, though not human killers. As we write poison gun wielding robots are being let loose on the Great Barrier Reef, where they will track down and kill starfish that are themselves destroying the reef. Once let loose no human will issue kill commands, the AIs will decide for themselves what lives and what dies.

These examples arguably show AI in control in limited, but significant, parts of life on earth, but to truly dominate the world, movie style, these individual AIs would need to start working together to create a synchronised AI army. That bossy self-service till needs to talk to your health monitor and as a result deny selling you beer. Both might then gang up with a credit scoring system to only raise your credit limit if you both buy a pair of trainers with a built-in GPS tracker, and only eat the kale from your smart fridge. The fridge of course will only open after the shoe data has shown you completed the required five mile run.

It's a worrying picture, but fortunately it's probably an unlikely one. Engineers worldwide are developing the *Internet of Things*, networks connecting all manner of devices and physical objects together to create new services. These are pieces of a jigsaw that would need to join together and form a big picture for total world domination. It's an unlikely situation — too much has to fall into place and work together. It's a lot like the infamous plot-hole in the film 'Independence Day' where an Apple Mac and an alien spaceship's software inexplicably have cross-platform compatibility, and just work when plugged together.

Our earthly AI systems are written in a range of computer languages, hold different data in different ways and use different and non-compatible rule sets and learning techniques. Unless we design them to be compatible, there is no reason why adding two safely designed AI systems, developed by separate companies for separate services would spontaneously blend to share capabilities and form some greater common goal without human intervention. Of course globalisation means that there is a big push to harmonise things by modern global, mega-sized companies out to make more profit by dominating the market...

So could AIs, and the robot bodies containing them, pass the test and take over the world? Arguably only if we clever, but puny, humans let them, and help them a lot. And why would we? Perhaps because humans are the stupid ones?

Chapter 9

Grids, Graphics and Games

Grids and games can matter. Grids form the basis of many games. They also matter a lot in computing. They are a way to represent images, for example, and a grid-based game about life even led to a whole new way to do computing. Rules for another grid-based game will help us explain why humans are no longer the best game players on the planet. Computer scientists are even now turning life itself into a game.

Grids and Games as Images

Games as a high-tech art industry

The history of computer games is fairly short, but the industry has already grown to a point where it is actually worth more than the film industry. Whether playing a troll in Warcraft or fighting those pesky pigs with some Angry Birds, computer games are based on computer code that sits inside our game stations or laptops, and our smartphones or tablets as we carry them around the world. They provide us with both entertainment and new ways to interact with other people.

Full video games can be divided into two main categories. Large games employ many hundreds of people: coders, designers and artists all working together to create the game. They use science too, for example in *physics engines*, the name for the clever pieces of computer software that run the physics of the game world. These engines decide how boulders drop or cloth blows in the wind. They are of course an example of **computational modelling**, modelling the world for the sake of fun though, rather than understanding. Video games today represent the fusion of computer science and art, as games pioneer *Richard Garriott* has said, they are the quintessential high-tech art.

The second main category of games, the independent games, are mostly developed for smartphones. They can be put together by a small number of dedicated creative coders and designers. The emergence of the smartphone app market has allowed an explosion of new ideas and themes to be explored and developed. This is especially so for games that integrate with social networks (our so-called *social graph*) that we all spend so much of our time on. Everyone has an idea for an app, they say, and given a little bit of help you can create one too. If you are interested, there are many free software packages available on the web that allow you to turn ideas into code for a smartphone. You can then download them to your phone and impress your friends.

Pixels makes pictures

At their core, most computer games are built on computer graphics and images (though watch out for more games in the future that you play in the real world with all your senses!) The images that we see on the screen are created from many thousands of *pixels*. Pixels are just picture elements: small points on the screen over which we have control of the brightness and colour **represented** by numbers. With a large enough screen, we can create any image we can imagine simply by setting the pixel values on the screen to the correct numbers. The more pixels we have, the higher the *resolution* and so the more detailed and clear the image can be. Figure 54(a) shows an image of a robot head with only 64 (i.e., 8×8) pixels. It is barely recognisable as there aren't enough pixels to show the detail. Figure 54(b) shows the same image but with 256 (i.e., 16×16) pixels. It is now clearly a robot head. With even more pixels, so higher resolution, the image could be even more detailed, perhaps showing

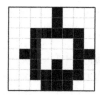

(a) A pixel image of a robot's head with only 8×8 pixels.

(b) A pixel image of a robot's head with 16×16 pixels.

Figure 54: Pixelated images at different resolutions.

the shape of the eyes, nose and mouth, rather than being just blobs, for example.

The screen of the computer itself can be thought of as a grid, and a game is then just a series of pictures that we control (more examples of **representations** in action).

There are a whole range of ways we can create these images: the *computer graphics*. In simple *raster* methods, we store the values for each pixel. Our first picture can be stored as 64 numbers:

00001000,00001000,00111110,00100010,
01100011,00101010,00111110,00011100

where a 0 means a white pixel and a 1 means a black pixel. We create images by moving along each line from top to bottom of the screen rapidly setting the pixel values.

The more pixels, the clearer the picture, but also the more numbers that need to be stored to **represent** the image. To store the higher resolution picture of the robot, we need 256 numbers instead of just 64:

0000000000000000,0000000010000000,
0000000111000000,0000000010000000,
0000011111110000,0000011111110000,
0000100000001000,0001101010101100,
0001100010001100,0001100000001100,
0000100111001000,0000100111001000,
0000100000001000,0000011111110000,
0000001000100000,0000001111100000.

In these images, we only have two digits to choose between per pixel, 1 and 0, so our images are only two colours: black and white. If we use more numbers each representing different colours, then we could store colour pictures in a similar way. That takes more numbers though.

An alternative **representation** is to store an image as the lines and shapes that make it up. In these so-called *vector* methods, we define the start and end points of thousands of lines and draw them rapidly on the screen. For example, to draw a square, rather than spelling out each pixel in the whole grid, you store a series of instructions such as:

Line (North, 50)
Line (East, 50)
Line (South, 50)
Line (West, 50)

To draw the image we just follow the instructions. This **representation** takes far less space in general, but has another big advantage too. The above draws a square of size 50. Suppose we want the image 10 times as big. We can just multiply all the lengths by 10 as we draw. If we want the square to be 10 times smaller we just divide the lengths by 10. With this **representation**, we can blow an image up as large as we like, to display on a bigger screen say, without having to store any more data, and without losing accuracy.

That is why **representations** of diagrams like that used in pdf files use less space and look just as good when you zoom into them. They are storing vector versions. A jpeg image on the other hand needs more memory to store a higher resolution image, and you need to decide the resolution of the grid when you save it. That's why, when you zoom into a jpeg image, things get blurry and lines get jagged.

Using vector methods, we can make 3D shapes by adding together, often tens of thousands of, simple so-called *graphic primitives*: spheres, cubes, cylinders, and so on. Different combinations allow us to create the complex shapes we want.

There are systems that simulate the transition of light rays in a synthetic world (more **computational modelling**, this time of how sources of light illuminate objects) to give photo realistic images. We can also attach complex movement scripts, often created by capturing the movements of real actors, to our graphic primitives to instruct the shape to move in the way we want. The limits are the amount of computing power available to do all the calculations, the quality of the code that coders can write to produce ever more natural looking graphics, and the imagination of the creative human mind. But even a simple grid and some easy coding rules can give rise to some fascination results.

The Game of Life

Gaming on the grid

Let's start simple, with a game based on a square grid, and a set of rules on how to switch pixels on or off. Switching a pixel's value depends on how many pixels are on in the area round it. Doesn't sound very exciting does it? Well think again. Even using this simple sort of game interesting things happen, and we can also use it to understand something about the natural world.

Mathematician *John Conway*'s *Game of Life*, as this game is called, was first published in 1970 and became a popular activity of computer scientists around the globe. The rules are simple, though it took Conway a great deal of effort to balance them correctly, so that interesting things happened.

The grid represents a simple square world, with *cells* (pixels) that can be on (alive) or off (dead). Each cell has a local neighbourhood made of the eight cells immediately adjacent horizontally, vertically and diagonally. To survive, an existing living cell needs to have exactly two or three live neighbour cells: enough of a supporting population but not too much. If any live cell has less than two live neighbour cells, the cell dies due to under-population. Similarly, any live cell with more than three live neighbours dies because of over-crowding. Finally, any empty cell with exactly three live neighbour cells springs into life, mimicking the process of reproduction. This is summarised in the *production rules* in Figure 55. Figure 56 shows an example pattern and one cycle of life.

From this simple mathematics, a simple set of production rules applied to the cells of the grid, strange and interesting patterns appear and vanish as time on the grid clicks on by, and cells live and die by the rules.

Play at life yourself

You can try it for yourself. You need a large grid. A chess board will do to start but you will quickly find you need a bigger grid. A Go board is better if you have one. Alternatively, draw out a large grid of squares on the biggest piece of paper you can find. Ideally, it should be infinite in size but that won't fit in your bedroom... so at some point you just have to accept that if your patterns get to the

EMPTY CELLS:
> **IF** exactly 3 cells adjacent
> **THEN** cell is BORN
> **ELSE** cell STAYS EMPTY

FULL CELLS:
> **IF** 2 or 3 cells adjacent
> **THEN** cell STAYS ALIVE
> **ELSE** cell DIES

Figure 55: The rules of the Game of Life.

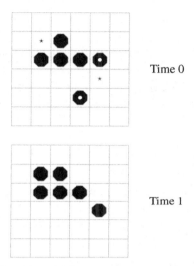

Time 0

Time 1

Figure 56: Applying the rules of life to an example. This shows one cycle of life and the result. Octagons show existing live cells. Small black stars show where life will be born, and a white circle marks a cell that will die.

edge of the board, you will need either to create some more board quickly, or that is the end of Life, as your creatures will fall off the end of the universe.

You need some counters for cells that come to life. It also helps to have some way to mark ones that are about to die in the next round. You can't just remove them as you need to work out everything. Go pieces are one possibility— swap black pieces for white pieces to show ones about to die (and go to heaven). You also need a way to mark squares where life is about to be born. Smaller pieces (perhaps beads) of some other colour can be used for this. You could use three kinds of coin or coloured beads (but you may need a lot of them if life takes off in your world).

Now all you do is place pieces on the board in a random pattern, then follow slavishly the laws of Life. They are your world's equivalent to the laws of physics. Work out all the births and deaths, swapping in the new pieces, across the whole board, before removing dying pieces and swapping living pieces for the cells being born, ready for the next round. To play Life, you need lots of attention to detail.

Make a mistake in a cell and you will end up with a totally wrong pattern.

There are also lots of online simulations, so search the web to see life in action on a bigger scale. If you can program of course then you could create your own version. The Oxford online Turtle system (www.turtle.ox.ac.uk/) includes a Game of Life program if you want to see how its done.

A menagerie of life

Conway found that some patterns were static. They remained in the same place on the grid, unchanged, so he called them *still life*, such as the snake in Figure 57. How many other simple starting patterns can you find that are still life?

Some patterns change shape through a fixed set of sub-patterns, and eventually come back to the starting pattern, only to then start again in an endless repeating loop. They were dubbed *oscillators*. For example, a really simple oscillator is the blinker shown in Figure 58. Start with collections of blinkers just far enough apart that they can't disrupt each other and you can make wonderful flashing patterns. The patterns formed from a cluster of oscillators like this are called *pulsars*, named after the exotic stars that produce regular pulses of energy.

A colleague of Conway, *Richard Guy*, came across starting shapes that stayed in the same pattern but moved across the grid. These were named *gliders* (see Figure 59). More generally, patterns that move like this are called *spaceships*.

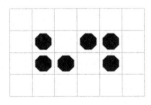

Figure 57: A snake: one form of still life in the Game of Life. Every cell containing a piece has 2 or 3 neighbours so no cells die. No empty cell has exactly 3 pieces around it so there are no births.

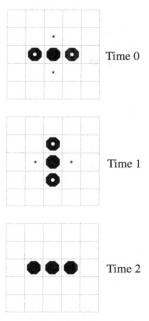

Figure 58: A blinker: one form of oscillator in the Game of Life. The cells above and below the centre piece, have 3 pieces next to them so are born, but at the same time each end cell dies as it is only next to one piece.

It is even possible to simulate logic gates in the Game of Life. As we've seen, they are the basic components of a computer. They can be made of transistors, neurons and now from the cells of the Game of Life. That means with a big enough grid you could create a working computer on the grid, just by the cells following those simple rules.

Modelling whole new worlds

Computer scientists started coming up with new variations of the game: three-dimensional grids, a hexagonal grid, and so on. By changing the grid world and the rules, they found ever more interesting patterns emerged as time passed on the grids and the computer repeated, iterating each step.

What Conway had invented came to be called *cellular automata*: another new way of doing computing. You could adapt the rules so

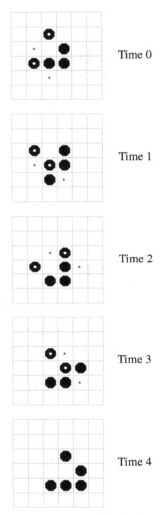

Figure 59: A glider. After four cycles of life, it returns to the original shape but having moved diagonally down the grid.

that the cells would do different kinds of computation. The simple cells with their simple rules could be changed and even made more complex. Each cell would now be an *automata*, sitting at a position on the grid and containing code with its own set of rules. When the automata came in contact with data placed onto the grid, the automata would munch through its data and that of the surrounding neighbourhood producing the appropriate output. This output might also depend on the past few (10 say) states of the cell. Conway's original rules were thrown out of the digital window.

These sorts of complex automata have all sorts of uses. They can be set up to look at the natural world, exploring how plants spread in a rain forest, how coral reefs develop, how seismic events occur and how animals migrate. Each cell becomes an **abstraction** of a small square of the world, coding rules for the behaviour of the thing of interest and how it interacts with those around it. Cellular automata have become a new way to study ecology via cell-based **computational modelling**.

Cellular automata can also help us understand how traffic jams form on our roads and disease spreads in a population. In cryptography, the data to be encrypted can be placed on a grid and then processed by the automata. They have rules that are simple to follow, so anyone can encrypt a message, but hard to reverse unless you know the secret key. That makes it hard to go back from the coded message to the original. Cellular automata have even been used to help compose music, too, and to do lots more besides. Not bad for something that started out as a simple game on a simple board.

The Games People Play

Fancy a game of words?

Conway's game didn't involve the standard two players, that competitive edge that we often want from our gaming. Here's a simple word game called Spit-Not-So for you to try (no actual spitting involved you will be glad to know). First the rules. Write down the words:

SPIT, NOT, SO, AS, IF, IN, PAN, FAT, FOP.

The game is played as follows:

1. The first player chooses a word from the list, crosses it out and writes it down.

2. The second player then does the same thing with a word not yet crossed out.
3. The players take turns to do this until one person wins. The winner is the first player to hold three words containing the same letter.

An example game might go:

Player 1 takes NOT
Player 2 takes SPIT
Player 1 takes FAT
Player 2 takes PAN
Player 1 takes FOP
Player 2 takes IF
Player 1 takes SO

... and wins holding NOT, FOP and SO. They have three words containing the letter O.

Play a few games to get the idea. Then read on to find out a sneaky way to win ... or maybe you can work it out yourself first. We will come back to it later.

HINT: Think about how you might arrange the words in a square to make it easier to spot winning sets of words. It's actually the same game as one you already know.

Out-smarting people

We know computers do some miraculous things and one of them is to out-smart people at games. A computer can beat the world champion at Chess, but how?... and could even a piece of paper act intelligently enough to play a game as well as humans? Yes. If it has the right rules, and now is your chance to play against that piece of paper and see.

A popular grid-based game for a quick bit of competitive gaming fun with pencil and paper is Noughts and Crosses (Tic-Tac-Toe) so let's play that to explore the basics of how computers can get into gaming themselves. In Noughts and Crosses, players take it in turns to make a move on a 3 × 3 board. One person plays O and the other X. A move just involves writing an X or O in an empty square of the

First of all I am X and I go first.

Move 1: I want to go in a corner.

Move 2: If you did not go there then I want to go in the opposite corner to my move 1. Otherwise I want to go in a free corner.

Move 3: If there are two Xs and a space in a line (in any order) then I want to go in that space. Otherwise if there are two Os and a space in a line then I want to go in that space. Otherwise I want to go in a free corner.

Move 4: If there are two Xs and a space in a line (in any order) then I want to go in that space. Otherwise if there are two Os and a space in a line then I want to go in that space. Otherwise I want to go in a free corner.

Move 5: I want to go in the free space.

Figure 60: This piece of paper plays perfect noughts and crosses. Just follow its instructions.

board. The first player to get three in a line, horizontally, vertically or diagonally wins. If no one does, then it is a draw.

You will struggle to beat the page of the book containing Figure 60! Try. Whenever it's the paper's turn to move just do what it tells you it wants to do in its instructions in the figure. Then you make whatever move you want to make. The paper gets to go first and is X.

Did the paper win? Was it a draw? Did you manage to out play the paper?

The best you could have managed (if you didn't cheat) was a draw. Did the paper play a respectable game? It had some gameplay knowledge, it was able to act intelligently. Much like Conway's Game of Life was based on rules, winning this game also works using a carefully designed and tested set of instructions, a now familiar algorithm, instructions that normally are stored in computer memory for the computer to follow.

Computers can only do the things the programmer thought of though. If things aren't as expected, it won't seem so clever. We wrote the above rules expecting the paper to go first... what if the paper has to play second? Try it! Does it still seem so clever? That is the skill of the programmer: writing rules for every eventuality. You might want to have a go at writing some good instructions for Player 2. Put them together with our piece of paper and it will be unbeatable.

Is this really intelligence, though? It is just following rules someone else wrote. Perhaps it is just the result that matters. It can certainly play as well as the best humans and is unbeatable, playing first at least. For more complex games, like chess, the algorithms need to be more sophisticated, but the idea is the same. For this algorithm, a human devised the precise way to play. Chess is too complicated for a human to spell out the rules of winning, though. So chess playing computers need an algorithm that tells them how to work it out for themselves.

Computers can now beat chess grand masters at their own game. We used to think that chess was the ultimate test of computer intelligence. In fact, if you have a complex enough and fast enough program with enough memory, so that for any particular board position the computer can work through the thousands and thousands of possible patterns of moves that are possible, they can then just select the one giving the best future positions and so beat a human player. This is called *tree search*. It is the algorithm we followed to come up with the perfect Noughts and Crosses instructions. There are too many possibilities in chess to do this exhaustively though. Chess computers look lots of moves ahead but not right to the end of the game. Good human chess players don't just work exhaustively step by step. They look for familiar patterns in the pieces and use these to select the strategy to play at that time. They play by **pattern matching**.

There are now more complex board based games that are the new challenges for computers to play well, such as the ancient game of Go. Unlike chess, Go, a popular two player game of strategy played with black and white counters on a 19 by 19 grid, has simple rules. However, the number of possible board conditions is massive, and needs larger effort than the number of atoms in the universe to analyse the way we have been talking about so far. Computers can't win it by playing the way they play chess.

The approach researchers took to winning Go was therefore different from the methods used in chess, where the computer had been explicitly programmed to play well. To beat a human expert at Go the computer program, *AlphaGo*, was programmed to learn as it went along, using a powerful general-purpose learning algorithm, using the ideas we've already seen. AlphaGo's algorithm extracted winning patterns from the games it played, improving its skill each time it either won or lost. Eventually, in 2015, after a lot of learning, AlphaGo was able to beat a professional Go expert in a multi-game tournament. In 2016, it beat one of the best human players in the world, *Lee Sedol*, 4–1 in a five game tournament. Chalk up another success for game play artificial intelligence (AI).

There are other types of games to play that aren't played on a board though: Poker, for example. *Pokerbots* are programs that play Poker. They can beat humans, but have to be able to deal with a different kind of game complexity. Unlike in Chess and Go, where everything is visible, Poker is a game of incomplete information. You do not know the cards other players have or the cards to be dealt. Pokerbots often use probability to make their best guesses, much like skilled poker players. Research in this field helps scientists better understand the way we humans deal with risks and decision making.

Polishing the game we play

Explicitly written AI rule sets like our algorithm for Noughts and Crosses, pop up all the time in real games. They often work in the background in computer versions of board games, so you can play against the computer. In multiplayer games, there are often non-player characters, characters that have artificial intelligence rules built in that control the way they interact with the real, human players, making the gameplay interesting and believable. AIs often also monitor the human player's performance to keep the game challenging, and control the generation of game elements like the difficulty of a level. Sometimes the intelligence sits in other places behind the scenes, for example understanding what type of phone and screen size you are loading the app onto, or checking that your network connection is working as well as it can. They can also collect data on how players actually play the game, what parts they play most and least, and what causes them to stop playing or is too difficult for the majority. All that data allows the game developers to adjust the gameplay, or improve the way in game purchases are taken up by players

How to win at Spit-Not-So

Let's return to that word game, Spit-Not-So. It's quite hard to keep track of what words are going to win in the game, unless you know this trick. Arrange the words in a square like the one in Figure 61 (make sure your opponent can't see them). Cross the words out as you play, using an X for your moves and an O for the other player.

Play a few games. It's now much easier to keep track of where to go. If you get a line of three, then you will find you have three of the same letters. If your opponent has any two in a line, they will win if you don't stop them getting the third. You are now just playing noughts and crosses, while your opponent struggles with Spit-Not-So. The two games are exactly the same — the same rules for perfect playing apply!

The positions of the words in the square are important. They are arranged so that words containing the same letter are in a line. That means that picking three words with the same letter now involves looking for lines (a visual pattern) not reading words. If you know how to play, the perfect game of noughts and crosses (using the instructions — the algorithm — given earlier) you should never be beaten at Spit-Not-So either. One algorithm wins at both games.

NOT	IN	PAN
SO	SPIT	AS
FOP	IF	FAT

Figure 61: How to arrange the words in a game of Spit-Not-So to make it easier to play.

We have of course just pulled that computational thinking trick we did with the tour guide puzzles: spotting when one problem, with a change of **representation**, is the same as one we have already solved. We can then pull out the algorithmic solution of the original to solve the new problem. The problems **generalise** to the same thing and so the solutions do too.

The way we see things

Why does the grid make the game easier to play for a human than when the words are in a list? The difference is just that the information has been presented in a way that makes it easier for our brains to process it. Our brains are very good at seeing visual patterns — we do it with very little effort (we will return to this in the next chapter). Much less effort is needed than searching for letters and remembering words in lists. The way that information is structured and presented to people matters. This is another example of why choosing an appropriate **representation** for data matters. It turns a difficult task into an easy one.

That is one of the reasons why *graphical user interfaces* are an improvement on the old systems of typing in commands. In a graphical user interface, you are processing information visually rather than having to work with words. The **pattern matching** to find the right thing to do is visual pattern matching, rather than being one about processing and understanding words.

Games these days have to give consideration to the user experience. Apps for example need to catch your attention and be easy to play straight away, or they get deleted. By ensuring that as a designer you understand the way our brains work, and by testing making sure you have got it right, you can make sure that the way into and around your game is easy and intuitive for the player.

Games, games everywhere

Conway's Life is a game, but real life is being turned into a game too. The philosophy and popularity of games has now reached out to other applications, through the idea of *gamification*. Gamification applies game elements and principles in new and different places, in an attempt to make people engage in things like education, physical exercise, office productivity and even to counter voter apathy.

The techniques build on the natural desire of many of us for competition, mastery of a skill, achievement or status amongst our friends. The games can include 'players' working together or in competition, to gain rewards including points, achievement badges, virtual currency or levelling up. By making the rewards each person has gained visible to the others, such as by providing leader boards, players are encouraged to compete on tasks. However, this explicit competitive element its not to everyone's taste, so many gamification applications simply focus on making the activity fun for the user, making it feel game-like.

There are also games that while fun to play actually help in accomplishing important scientific and cultural tasks. Examples of these include games that help sort massive amounts of data about the shapes of galaxies, help in medical drug development, or in the cataloguing of ancient manuscripts. Other games help tag pictures on the web with good descriptions so partially sighted people can understand the images. These games crowd source intelligence, and use the human players' skills to help the computers sort out the complex data it has to process. Human brains still do that better.

Even if computers can beat the best human players at games like chess and go, there are still some games that humans play best (for now). They tend to be ones that aren't just played on grids, but are closer to living a real life.

Chapter 10

Seeing the Wood and the Trees

Pattern matching is at the heart of computational thinking, and patterns are everywhere. Computer scientists need to be good at seeing patterns, but also to be good at building algorithms that work with patterns. We can understand the ideas by looking at pattern matching in the algorithms behind mind reading magic tricks. Using generalisation in the form of mathematical theorems, we can devise both tricks and other algorithms that we can be sure work. The same ideas are central in the powerful algorithms that allow computers to see the world as well as humans can. By creating algorithms that can both discover and then use patterns, we can create ever more useful programs. We are teaching computers to do computational thinking so they can do human things as well as we can.

Mind Reading Magic

Seeing patterns everywhere

How many times have you looked at the clouds on a summer's day and seen fluffy animals, or discovered the face of a film star celebrity looking back at you out of a burst fried egg on your breakfast plate? Both are examples of our brain trying to find patterns in the world around us. In these cases, though our brains are finding patterns that arise simply by chance, other patterns our brains spot are more important. They may even be keeping us alive.

Finding and predicting patterns are arguably our brain's main job, whether it's trying to find the patterns in sight to let us see objects, or in sounds to let us hear words. Other patterns are involved in planning the decisions and actions we take. Those decisions are based on our knowledge of the patterns about what has happened before. We also like patterns. We feel comfortable with them. The TV news follows a pattern, for example: they tell us what's coming up, they show us, they then remind us what they have shown... three stages we want to experience to feel comfortable in our viewing.

Literature is filled with recurring patterns that we enjoy and feel familiar with. The *monomyth*, is an idea of writer and mythologist, *Joseph Campbell* from 1949, that embodies a familiar pattern followed by the journeys of heroes. It appears in stories and movies both in the modern day and through history. The pattern involves the individual going on an adventure, facing a major challenge, overcoming it and returning home a changed person. This pattern, with its dramatic three part structure of start, middle and conclusion, occurs in literature like Homer's Odyssey, much of Shakespeare, and Tolkien's Lord of the Rings. It is also the basis of movies like Star Wars and Indiana Jones. The pattern seems to structure stories so that we find them pleasing, easy to follow and fulfilling.

We've seen that pattern matching is at the heart of computational thinking, too. It's used both in spotting **abstractions** and **generalisation**, coming up with production rules and choosing good **representations**. Computer scientists are also interested in understanding the best ways to find and predict patterns. They apply computational thinking to invent the best ways to do **pattern matching** itself, and the results often find their way into our world in the form of complex pattern finding algorithms. They are implemented on computers, allowing the machines to do **pattern matching** themselves. Computational thinking is applied to the ideas behind computational thinking itself.

These **pattern matching** algorithms might be looking at patterns in the chemical bases that make up our genetic data, trying to match them with patterns of particular types of disease in patients. They might be trying to predict fluctuations in the financial markets to give a competitive edge. Perhaps they are predicting how graphical characters in computer games should respond to the patterns detected in your playing style with an aim of keeping you interested. They may even be letting machines 'see' the world like we do. Why shouldn't machines see animals in the clouds too! Patterns are everywhere, its just a matter of finding them.

Magical matching: codes and conjuring

Let's look at a some simple **pattern matching** algorithms to get the idea. Magicians realised long ago that if they know a secret pattern that you don't then they can use it to create magical effects. There is long proud history of two-person mentalism acts, for example. A member of the magician's team is blindfolded on stage while another selects objects from the audience. Through a 'shared mental link' the blind-folded person on stage then reveals what the objects are, despite being blindfolded. This is done using clever word codes, and takes a great deal of memory work for the two performers.

For example, if the chosen object was a pen, the helper might ask "Right, what do I have in my hand?" If a pocket watch was offered, the question asked might instead be "What object do I have in my hand? Think carefully. Take your time". Of course, these are rather suspicious examples: the magicians would be much more subtle, making the rules harder to remember. This type of entertainment proved very popular in its day and more and more elaborate verbal codes were developed by the performers, a pattern hidden in plain sight in the words spoken that when decoded on stage made the impossible happen.

Read minds yourself

You can experiment with the power of hidden patterns by doing a bit of mind reading yourself. This version doesn't need quite such a good memory as the traditional performance. You will need a willing accomplice, a partner who is in on the act, and a room full of spectators. The act, and do take time to make it seem magical and mysterious, involves one of the team, the magician, leaving the room. The audience then secretly select an item in the room that must be discovered by the magician when they return.

The assistant, stays in the room when the choices are made to "ensure fair play and that no one changes their minds". Once the magician has returned, the assistant wanders around in a seemingly random way and points to various object asking a single identical question each time: "Is this the selected object?" The magician is able to correctly answer yes or no each time.

Rather than memorise a complex pattern of verbal codes to accomplish this effect, you can use a simple **pattern matching** based predictive algorithm. Agree with the assistant on some object in advance, a lamp perhaps. Whatever you choose, let's call it x. The secret signal is that when the assistant points to that object, then the next one pointed to, let's call it y, will be the chosen object. The shared secret is the shared algorithm in Figure 62. Of course, you both need to agree in advance what x is.

If you are asked to do the trick again, attempting to guess a series of objects, this pattern may become too obvious. It's easy to get round this by applying a little bit of computational thinking and extending the algorithm. Each time you do the trick, you use a different object to point to before pointing to the selected object: a lamp, then the carpet, then the light switch, for example. x now changes each time. The code you both work out could look something like the one in Figure 63.

You should of course be sure that there is a lamp, a carpet and a light switch by the door before you begin. You then point to the lamp when attempting to guess the first object (when the number of the attempt is 1), the carpet for the second (when the number of the attempt is 2) and the light switch for the third (when the number of the attempt is 3). The final default, catch all, statement is there in case you are asked to find a fourth object, or even a fifth, or sixth. Some people are never satisfied! You haven't prepared for these, but good **algorithmic thinking** says you should cover every

1. Assistant points to a series of random things
2. Assistant points to x
3. Assistant points to the audience's selected item, y
4. Magician says "It was y" and takes applause

Figure 62: The mind reading algorithm.

1. Assistant points to a series of random things
2. IF (number of the attempt is 1)
    THEN
    > 1. Assistant points to lamp
    > 2. Assistant points to chosen object, *y*
    > 3. Magician says "It was *y*" and takes applause

    ELSE IF (number of the attempt is 2)
    > 1. Assistant points to carpet
    > 2. Assistant points to chosen object, *y*
    > 3. Magician says "It was *y*" and takes applause

    ELSE IF (number of the attempt is 3)
    > 1. Assistant points to light switch by door
    > 2. Assistant points to chosen object, *y*
    > 3. Magician says "It was *y*" and takes applause

    DEFAULT
    > 1. Magician says
    > > "My psychic powers are drained.
    > > I'm sorry. I can't go on"

Figure 63: An extended mind reading algorithm.

eventuality. Therefore, you have a default excuse ready should they push beyond your prepared-for cases for doing three mind miracles: "My psychic powers are drained. I'm sorry. I can't go on."

When the patterns don't match what plan can you hatch?

This **pattern matching** algorithm will in most cases allow you to perform magic to entertain, but once in a while there might be problems. The logic in our thinking needs to be perfect, down to every detail. We may think, for example, that we've covered every eventuality, but what happens if the second object selected by the audience is in fact the lovely room's carpet, which you want to use as your secret cue? The **pattern matching** algorithm has a problem. This is something unexpected that we didn't plan for in the algorithm. It says you must point to the carpet then point to the carpet again! Not very magical?

Of course, when performing the magic trick you, being human, can think on your feet, and work your way round that with a bit of humour, doing a double point to the carpet, then joking about it. If you had programmed a robot magician to do the trick, though it would just follow the algorithm exactly, and look silly. It would only make a joke of it, if you'd realised the problem might happen, and added appropriate joke-making code to the algorithm.

Ok, so it's not the end of the world for a robot magician to mess up, but if this sort of problem arose in, say, a **pattern matching** algorithm for deciding that all the various elements had been done in the right order to trigger the safe deployment of an aircraft's landing gear, that's a different story. Being sure you have thought through all the possibilities and have built-in pattern matching for them is trickier than you might think, but programmers have to get it right if their software is to work.

There are a whole range of patterns that we need to be sure we can find and respond correctly to in what we call safety-critical systems, like hospital software, control of nuclear reactors or the next generation of self-driving cars. Just having a load of possible cases won't cover everything, so computer scientists use **logical** and **analytical thinking** and build mathematical ways to understand these systems, for example, based on the ideas we saw for solving the puzzles in Chapter 4. Mathematics gives us a more robust tool to understand the patterns in the system. Then computer scientists write programs that do the **logical thinking** based on the maths. Computers are much better at exploring all the possibilities without missing any than we are. The computers are doing yet more computational thinking for us.

Prime Magic

A prime pattern for a feat of mathematical magic

Let's look now at a different type of pattern matching magic trick, one we know will always (always, always, always) work because we know the mathematics of the patterns behind it ensures it does. Maths itself is all about spotting and understanding patterns in things, then turning that into general facts that mathematicians call theorems: the computational thinking idea of **generalisation** again (the basics of computational thinking are drawn from all over the place). Maths and magic go well together, as once mathematicians and computer scientists have spotted patterns, magicians can weave magic from them.

Ask three friends to each enter a random number into their calculators (or mobile phones if they include a calculator). Tell them you will be able to predict numbers that will exactly divide their chosen random number. They can choose absolutely any three digit number on the calculator. It is their choice. They should keep it hidden from you, though.

Pretend to get premonitions from each of them, saying that with just three digits its too easy. To make it harder, they should each use a larger number. So to make it easier for them and harder for you, they should enter the same three digit number again to give a personal six digit number. For example, if they entered 345 initially their new personal number would be 345345.

You focus all your psychic powers, and are then able to instantly tell each of them a different small number that will exactly divide their personal six digit number; you confidently state that although you could not possibly know the entered random numbers, the first friend's number is exactly divisible by 7, the second by 11 and the final one by 13. There will be no remainder. They each perform the division on their calculator, to check and show you are right. As you predicted, there is no remainder.

For the final part of the trick you say you will instantly calculate a six digit number that is exactly divisible by the three small numbers you already gave, three 'random' numbers derived from your friends initial free choices. You tell them this six digit number and again the calculator shows you have been able to correctly calculate the appropriate number in your head.

Magic-ing patterns out of randomness, or is it?

The secret of the trick is that the three small numbers you call out are always 7, 11 and 13. The rest of the trick is self-working: an algorithm.

The trick relies on the mathematical fact that entering any three digit number followed by the same three digits again is mathematically exactly the same as multiplying the original three digit number by 1001. Why? If you multiply a number by 1000, then you put three zeros on the end. In computer science terminology, you shift it three places. Multiplying by 1001 means multiply by 1000 and then add the number back on. That last addition just replaces the three zeros by the original number.

For example, 345,345 is 345×1001 (i.e., $345,000 + 345$). The small numbers you use in your predictions are 7, 11 and 13. Now $7 \times 11 \times 13 = 1001$. That means that when you double up any number like 345 in this way you are multiplying it by those three numbers. $345,345 = 345 \times 1001$ is just another way of saying $345,345 = 345 \times 7 \times 11 \times 13$. That means any of the three numbers will divide into the six digit number exactly, just cancelling that number back out of the total.

This mathematical fact makes the trick always work as long as you use the numbers 7, 11 and 13. They will divide exactly into any of your three friends' duplicated-digits personal numbers. The final part of the trick, showing your amazing mathematical powers, simply involves you giving any 6 digit number that is a repetition of any three digit number such as 765765. This will of course be divisible by 7, 11 and 13. It has to be because of the same mathematical principle. So the maths makes the trick work but your presentation makes it magical.

Spotting the pattern in the maths led to a **generalised** rule (the mathematical theorem) that can then be exploited in an algorithm, here to do magic, though in other situations it could be the basis of a program or hardware design. For example, hardware units that do fast multiplication, often do it by a similar trick, based on a similar theorem. You can quickly multiply numbers by two that are stored as binary by just shifting them left, i.e., sticking a 0 on the end. No actual multiplication required.

Prime Factors

7, 11 and 13 are *prime numbers*. That is, they are special numbers that nothing divides into except 1 and themselves. Check it: none of them divide by 2 exactly, none divide by 3, none divide by 4, and so on. These three numbers are called the *prime factors* of 1001. The prime factors of a positive whole number (i.e., an integer) are the prime numbers that divide that integer exactly.

An intriguing general fact that the Greek mathematician, *Euclid* worked out is that every integer greater than 1 that isn't a prime number itself can be obtained by multiplying prime numbers together. Furthermore, there is only one such set of prime numbers for each integer: the product is unique. This fact is called the *unique-prime-factorisation theorem*.

Applied to the number 1001 it tells us that some prime numbers do exist to make the trick work, and they will be the only prime numbers that it will work for: the only prime numbers that work are 7, 11 and 13.

Testing for patterns in the maths

Knowing the maths underneath tells us what happens if things change. For example, will the trick work for a single digit number: will it work if the initial number is 3, and the duplicated number 33? The answer is no. To duplicate up single digit numbers, we have to multiply by 11 rather than by 1001. The number 33 is 3 multiplied by 11. So far so good, but 11 is a prime number and that means nothing but 1 and 11 divide into it. We can't come up with more prime factors. It would only work for 11 and 1 and that's too obvious to be magical.

Will the trick work for a two digit duplicated number like 3434? The answer again is no, as 3434 is 34 multiplied by 101 and 101 is a prime number too. Knowing the maths lets us predict the patterns that will work, the patterns we should check for.

One way to make the trick even more foolproof is to get your friend to quickly read out their number, then you snap back instantly with a number that divides it. If they make a mistake and, for example, say 123 124, you can immediately correct them on that last 4 where they made a mistake, and still give the correct answer lightning quick. This is now **pattern matching** as part of a checking algorithm. You know what is expected and you check it's there.

Some safety-critical software does a similar thing. The programmers include assertions in the code of what they expect to be true when the program gets to that point. If the assertion, unexpectedly, isn't true, special code can run to deal with the problem. Entering numbers correctly often matters a lot, and if people enter invalid numbers its really important the software doesn't just ignore it, but points out the problem and lets the person correct it (unlike in our trick). These are just some of the many ways of writing software that is dependable that helps avoid disasters.

Patterns in pong: a smelly card trick

Here is another trick, that seems impossible and also is a bit of fun. It involves you finding an exception to a known mathematical pattern while hiding that pattern from your audience. It uses your ability "to find a card by the smell left on it by the person who selected it". Clearly, you need to be sensitive in the way you present this trick!

Get your spectator to shuffle the cards in a pack. This will imprint their scent on them. You then take the cards back stating that after the initial shuffle some cards are more engrained with body scent, some less. You run through the cards sniffing them rapidly one by one, dividing them into two approximately equal piles. One pile contains those with strong scents: these cards must have been in more hand contact in the shuffle. The other pile contains those that have no scent at all: they must have been missed in the shuffling.

Ask the spectator to randomly choose and remember one of the cards in the strong scent pile, keeping it secret from you. They should then slot it somewhere in the less smelly pile. You shuffle this pile, and then proceed to sniff each card again. Through smell alone, you manage to correctly find the card the spectator hid in the pile of less smelly cards.

The smell-free secret algorithm

The secret to this trick is all about setting up a pattern (the difference between the smelly and non-smelly cards) that isn't obvious, and being able to spot the exception to that pattern. The secret pattern is just the prime numbers. You put all the prime numbered cards in one pile, and the non-primes in the other. Let the Ace count as 1, Jack as 11, Queen as 12 and King 13 for this. Separating the primes involves splitting out the 2, 3, 5, 7, Jack and King into one pile and all the non-prime number cards in the other. 1 isn't a prime number by definition so the Aces go into the non-prime pile. Of course, it's nothing to do with smell. Its about using the card's numerical value as a pattern to separate them in a way that makes the difference between the piles visible to you but not to anyone else.

The rest of the trick just needs a confident performance from you and some simple pattern matching exception detection. Suppose the smelly pile is the non-prime cards, then you will be looking for a prime value card in the shuffled non-smelly pile. It will stick out like a big shiny needle in a haystack to you, but for your audience it will just look like a haystack.

Of course, there are other patterns you could use to define the differences between the piles, say red cards in one and black in another, or court cards in one and spot cards in another, but these would be too obvious. The patterns would be too clear to the audience, and the magic just wouldn't happen.

Really Seeing the World

Finding an edge to help computers see

Let's move to something a bit more complicated now: allowing computers to see. It isn't just about hooking up a camera. The computer needs to be able to identify things in the scene: spot patterns and then work out what object they match: what it is seeing. Only then can we really claim it can 'see'.

Finding patterns in pictures is something our brains do all the time. The light that enters our eye is converted by the retina at the back of our eyeballs into signals that run to the brain. This information is processed to find interesting patterns, shapes and eventually objects. We are still discovering more about how human vision works, but being able to give a computer or a robot the ability to see is an important and difficult technical challenge. It means we need to come up with algorithms to teach computers how to spot patterns in visual scenes. One of the fundamental things human brains seem to do, that allows us to recognise objects, is to find edges in images. They work out where the lines are. As we saw with *vector* images, lines are the first step to shapes and then objects. So how could a computer 'see' lines?

First of all let's consider a very, very boring picture (see Figure 64(a)). Like all pictures that computers use from cameras, it is digital and made up of *pixels*. Normally an image is made of thousands and thousands of pixels. The real world isn't made of pixels, of course! It is just a **representation** of the image. Each pixel has its place in the image and a particular colour or brightness value associated with it. Our boring picture has only 32 pixels, and two shades of grey, lighter grey and darker grey. But as you can see looking at it, it does have something interesting: a vertical edge where the picture steps from light grey on one side to dark grey on the other. The edge itself isn't actually a line of pixels though, it's

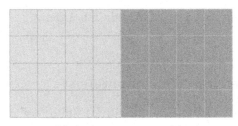

(a) An image to try and 'see'.

3	3	3	3	4	4	4	4
3	3	3	3	4	4	4	4
3	3	3	3	4	4	4	4
3	3	3	3	4	4	4	4

(b) The image represented as numbers.

Figure 64: An image and its representation.

only there in the difference between pixels. We can only see it as a thing because our brain is doing lots of processing.

If we are going to write algorithms to allow a computer to spot edges, we need a good **representation** for them to use. We can easily represent this image as a set of numbers, using different values for light and dark grey. That will make it easy for us to use maths in our processing algorithms. Let's decide that light grey is the number 3 and dark grey is the number 4. These numbers could be the amount of ink needed to print the pixel, for example. The image with just the naked numbers looks like the one in Figure 64(b).

The edge is still in there but it is now much harder for us humans to see. It exists in the pattern of numbers only, and we are not as naturally good at processing number patterns as images ones. As we will see, this **representation** will make it easier for a machine to process it though.

Now let's look at the even smaller, duller pattern of Figure 65. This new pattern is just three pixels long and, to be fair, it has a negative number in there which might help make it a bit more interesting. So how can this pattern help give simple sight to a computer? Computer scientists call this smaller pattern a *digital filter*. Like a normal filter for, say, making filter coffee, it only lets certain things through. In this case, it lets through number patterns rather than coffee.

To make a digital filter work, it is passed over an underlying set of numbers, multiplying itself, element by element, by the pattern under it. The results from each element of the filter are then added together to give the final output of the filter.

Let's see an example. Suppose the underlying input pattern of numbers representing the image is 3, 3, 3, 4, 4, 4. We can see how this works for the first three input numbers in Figure 66(a). We multiply the filter by the corresponding numbers, giving −3, 0 and 3, then

−1	0	1

Figure 65: A pattern to use as a digital filter.

Input	3	3	3	4	4	4
Filter	**−1**	**0**	**1**			
Multiply	$3 \times -1 = -3$	$3 \times 0 = 0$	$3 \times 1 = 3$			
Add		$-3 + 0 + 3 = 0$				
Filter Output		**0**				

(a) Applying the digital filter to the first position.

Input	3	3	3	4	4	4
Filter		**−1**	**0**	**1**		
Multiply		$3 \times -1 = -3$	$3 \times 0 = 0$	$4 \times 1 = 4$		
Add			$-3 + 0 + 4 = 1$			
Filter Output		**0**	**1**			

(b) Applying the digital filter to the second position.

Figure 66: Applying the digital filter to the image represented by 3, 3, 3, 4, 4, 4 (part 1).

add these together to give 0. That is the new value we place in the filter's output. The filter then moves along one element, as if it's on a conveyor belt. It settles over the new input numbers and calculates the next filter output giving us the result in Figure 66(b). Move along please! The filter shifts one step more to the right hovering over new input numbers and calculates the next filter output. That gives us the result in Figure 67(a). Finally, moving one more space to the right our hard working filter reaches the end, and produces its last output as in Figure 67(b).

What's in an image's patterns anyway?

After all that mathematics where are we now? Well let's look at what we have, ignoring the workings (see Figure 68).

In the output pattern, the filter has produced numbers that are higher only where there is a change in the values of the input sequence. Of course the output filter is a little bit smaller than the input image as the two end values are empty, but it is far more useful. Rather than consider these input values as numbers now, think of them as pixel values. They are a picture.

Input	**3**	**3**	**3**	**4**	**4**	**4**
Filter			**−1**	**0**	**1**	
Multiply			3 × −1 = **−3**	4 × 0 = **0**	4 × 1= **4**	
Add				−3 + 0 + 4 = **1**		
Filter Output		**0**	**1**	**1**		

(a) Applying the digital filter to a third position.

Input	**3**	**3**	**3**	**4**	**4**	**4**
Filter				**−1**	**0**	**1**
Multiply				4 × −1 = **−4**	4 × 0 = **0**	4 × 1= **4**
Add				−4 + 0 + 4 = **0**		
Filter Output		**0**	**1**	**1**	**0**	

(b) Applying the digital filter to the last position.

Figure 67: Applying the digital filter to the image represented by 3, 3, 3, 4, 4, 4 (part 2).

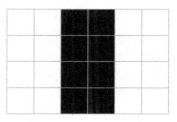

Figure 68: The overall result of applying the digital filter.

Figure 69: The result of applying the digital filter to the original image in Figure 64.

Now think what happens when you run this filter across a line of our first big boring image of Figure 64, then move down a row and run along the next line, and the next until you have filtered the whole input image. You will have a new, be it slightly smaller, image as in

Figure 69, where we have assumed number 0 is white and number 1 is black. It has a special property. All the areas where there were vertical edges are highlighted: they have become lines. Our boring image now has an actual line running down the middle. A simple bit of maths has extracted a more useful pattern from the initial image pattern. Edges have been turned into lines: the computer can start to see them.

Computer scientists have invented lots of different filters that can each find different things in images. The mathematical process underpinning them all is the same as the one we just went through. It is only the filters themselves that get more complicated. Each filter is a pattern. Using patterns in the filters to find patterns in an image is fundamental to computer vision. It also mimics what we know about the way we humans see, where it seems that cells in the brain are sensitive to particular patterns of changes in intensity of light like edges.

Things they are a-changin' too

Important patterns can exist over time too, as we try to build software that can follow people, facial expressions or objects as they move and change. To a computer, a video is just a big set of numbers. It is a set of pictures taken over a period of time, and as we've seen each picture is just a big bunch of numbers itself. All those numbers need to be filtered to find the interesting stuff. We can create filters that not only work in space but over time too. These so-called *temporal filters* are looking for similarities or differences in pixel values at particular places in video images as they change throughout the movie. If you think about our example filter $[-1, 0, +1]$, it works because it's a little compact **abstraction** of what we want to find, it has the simple characteristics of an edge: it starts low then it gets higher.

To follow more complex patterns in time, we sometimes don't know exactly what the pattern is, so it's hard to create an initial filter to be able to find it. To solve this problem, we normally use algorithms that learn the patterns we want to be able to find. This involves creating, often complicated, filters by taking hundreds of examples of the patterns we want to find. For example, we might take hundreds of videos of the normal behaviour of people getting on and off an underground train, extracting the most likely patterns from them. Then if we run these learnt filters on a live platform scene, they can alert us automatically to suspicious behaviours. They are patterns of movement that aren't what we would expect, like someone waiting too long at a platform edge, or a package that no one picks up: exceptions to the patterns we have learnt.

Similarly, time changing patterns are important in music. After all that's all that music is, notes that change over time in a pleasant way, based on interesting patterns. Filters can be used to help remove imperfections in musical recording. An example of this is the infamous auto tune software that turns shaky-singing pop stars into perfect sounding singers. It looks at the pattern of sound from the singer and the pattern of sound that should be there, and tweaks the singer's vocal signal to be more in line with what's needed. Music recognition services use *audio fingerprints*. They are just patterns of sound elements like frequencies, tempos and so on, extracted from a piece of music. They give a unique set of values, the music's fingerprint, which can be matched to the values in a massive data base of already labelled songs, to correctly identify an unknown piece.

Patterns in medicine and genetics can be learned too. We can potentially predict the diseases we might suffer from, knowing the patterns in our genes, or understand how our own particular gene patterns will make us interact with particular drugs so that treatment can be personally tailored. These applications of computer science and pattern discovery open up the possibility of new ways that medicine can both discover cures and work to make us better. In the future, your gene sequence might, for example, be taken when you enter hospital so that by the time you get to the ward you can be given drugs specifically designed for you, that ensure they minimise any side effect in you personally. This is all now a real possibility. It is all down to computers being given ways to do computational thinking themselves.

Patterns, predictions and patients and prisons

These sorts of applications can be incredibly useful, but as we saw in an earlier chapter, computer scientists, as they create their software, also need to be aware that the algorithms they create, the mathematics they invent, give machines abilities that could be abused. Ethics, the study or what's right or wrong, has a long standing and important place in human philosophy and legal history. Could a filter ever be designed that could predict from patterns in the data about them, that an individual was about to commit a crime? If so, would it be right to arrest them before the crime was committed? Should juries in legal cases be able to understand the strengths and weaknesses of mathematical and computing techniques increasingly being applied these days in the detection of supposed criminal behaviours? If the pattern in your genes says you are likely to suffer from a particular cancer in later life, would you want to know? Should insurance companies know and so charge you more for life insurance? And suppose your genes in childhood are tested and they show a pattern that suggests you will grow to be a violent criminal, what should be done? These are questions that are important and the answers are complex and difficult, but computer scientists must play their part in society and help others understand what they do and how they do it, otherwise it will just seem like magic to the outsider. And while magic is a great way to entertain and have fun, it's definitely not the right way to decide how our society evolves.

Chapter 11

Medical Marvels Inside Out

Modern healthcare relies on computer technology and the cunning computational thinking behind it. However, you need mathematicians and, scientists to come up with the basics first. The computer scientists and electronic engineers then create algorithms and electronics that turn the science and maths into technology that saves lives. Let's start with a game to see how.

A Slice of Life

Battleships, Beatles and body parts

In the last chapter, we suggested **pattern matching** might be the future of medicine. In this chapter, we look at some of the ways computers and so computational thinking already help save lives. The next time you are in hospital, either visiting someone or ill yourself, take a look around. The ward and the hospital are filled with the results of computational thinking. Whole departments in the hospital depend on computers processing data about you to be able to work. The CAT scan, ultrasound, cardiac implants... so much of today's healthcare is possible only because of the algorithms, sensors and computer devices. Someone had to write all the code to make those gadgets work.

Have you ever wondered how, for example, doctors can take pictures in slices through the body? Being able to see how the various parts in your body look in cross-section is a useful aid to diagnosis, but you can't slice someone open just to have a peak, you need to use technology to let you see inside. The story of how this important

Nobel Prize winning medical breakthrough became a medical reality involves some clever rediscovered maths, computers and a 60's rock group!

Me and my X-ray shadow

X-ray images are just photos taken by shining X-rays, rather than visible light, at objects to illuminate them. Because X-rays pass through soft tissue, but not denser material like bone and your organs, they take pictures of the inside of your body. In a normal X-ray, you stand in front of a photographic plate, and then X-rays shine through you onto the plate behind. Your bones, containing lots of calcium, have a higher density than the flesh and muscle surrounding it, so the bones absorb the X-rays. In effect, you get a bone shadow being cast on the photographic plate. Useful as X-rays are, the problem is that you only get to know how much bone an X-ray has gone through and nothing about where that bone was along the X-ray's journey. The shadow is flat, but your body is solid.

Digital shadows

Digital X-rays essentially do the same. They take a snapshot but using an array of digital sensors instead of a photographic (i.e., chemical) plate. Even digital X-ray machines can only give you flat images of the body's innards. Just like a shadow they squash all the depth details. Your insides are three-dimensional though, so it definitely would be useful to be able to slice through your body and get a proper 3D view. This is possible using a computer-based method called *tomography*, from the Greek tomos (slice) and graphia (describing). It still uses X-rays, but in tomography the X-ray source and the detector rotate round the body taking lots of images at different angles. It's like different shadows being cast as the sun moves round you. Imagine you are using tomography on a cylinder, and your X-ray source is a torch. Move the torch round the cylinder and look at the shadow cast on a piece of paper moving at the opposite side to the torch. Each shadow picture would look the same because a cylinder is circularly symmetric. Now imagine a more interesting shape, a teapot, say. Each of the shadow pictures would depend on where you were at the time in relation to the shape. With some clever maths, a reconstruction algorithm and a computer you can go from the shadow pictures back to the shape.

In tomography, these shapes are the organs and innards of your body, and they can be recorded in their full 3D glory. There are now systems that spiral the X-ray source round the body making it quicker. You can even do tomography at very high speed allowing slices through the beating heart to be calculated. The maths behind this technology, called the *Radon transform* after Czech mathematician *Johann Radon*, who died in 1956, was developed purely as an abstract mathematical theory. No one at the time could see any use for it!

Let's Play Battleships

Pencil and paper games

While you are wondering how we can actually turn those flat images back into a 3D scan of the body, let's take a break and play a game of Battleships. Battleships is another simple grid-based pencil and paper game. Using a square grid of paper, with the rows and columns labelled, you and a mate decide where on your grids you are going to position your 'fleet'. A fleet consists of a number of different types of ships: a battleship normally takes up four squares, either horizontally or vertically, a cruiser (a smaller type of ship), takes up say only two squares and destroyers are normally one square. At the start, you decide how many of each type of ship you will both have in a fleet, and secretly position them on your grid. The rules are that you take it in turns to 'fire' at your opponent's grid. For example, they might fire on position B9. That's the square in Row B and Column 9. If that grid location is a part of one of your ships, it's a hit. You have to admit it and say what type of ship it is, and then give your opponent another go. This way players can try and discover, for example, whether the four square battleship is positioned horizontally or vertically. The first player to sink all of the other person's fleet wins. Those single square destroyers are the

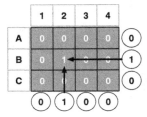

(a) A pond wars grid with a single destroyer.

	1	2	3	4	
A	0	0	0	0	0
B	0	1	0	0	1
C	0	0	0	0	0
	0	1	0	0	

(b) Using pond wars clues to determine where the destroyers are.

Figure 70: Pond Wars.

hardest to get of course, as you need to fire right on top of them to sink them.

Pond wars

Now imagine the much smaller game of battleships of Figure 70(a). Rather than an ocean, it's a pond. There is one destroyer (indicated by the number 1 in a sea of zeros) at grid location B2. You might be lucky and hit B2 on your first shot, or it may take a long process of elimination to find it. Is there another way you could find where the 1 is?

I see no ships, so give us a clue

The answer is yes, but only if you can get your opponent to give you some simple clues. Then you could work it out. First, get them to add up all the values along the rows and give you the answer for each row. For the pond of Figure 70(a), you would get the information: Row A is 0 (as its $0 + 0 + 0 + 0$ though you only give the total 0), Row B is 1 (as it's $0 + 1 + 0 + 0$) and Row C is 0. That is a start. You now know the ship is on Row B but you don't know where on Row B it is. Next, ask for the sum down the columns. Column 1 is 0, Column 2 is 1, Column 3 is 0 and Column 4 is 0. You now know it is in column number 2. This is shown in Figure 70(b), where we've put the clues in circles along the edges of the grid. Combining this information, gives you the location as being grid position B2, and BANG, its sunk!

A guide to automatic ship finding

Now suppose there are two destroyers somewhere in the grid. This time we aren't going to say where they are. Your friend gives you the sums along the rows and down the columns again. This time you are told that Row A is 2, Row B is 0 and Row C is 0; Column 1 is 1, Column 2 is 0, Column 3 is 1 and Column 4 is 0, as in Figure 71(a). Where are the ships?

Here is a general approach to finding the ships. First, we've been told that in Row A, the total is 2. There is something in there! We can spread the information that there is something in Row A all the way along that row. Though we have smeared the data along the row, we still don't know where the 'something' in Row A is, just that

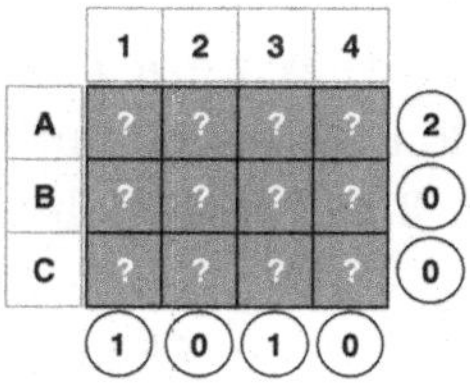

(a) A hidden pond wars grid with clues.

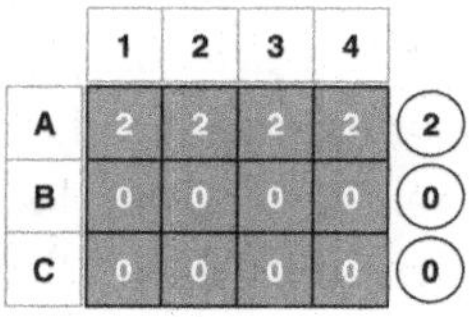

(b) Smearing all the row information across the rows.

Figure 71: Finding the destroyers in a pond war grid (part 1).

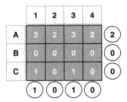

(a) Smearing all the column information up the columns.

(b) Combining the column and grid information.

Figure 72: Finding the destroyers in a pond war grid (part 2).

it's in there somewhere. Let's keep going. We do this smearing for Row B and Row C, too. Not much extra information here as they both had totals of zero. We are left with the grid of Figure 71(b).

We know there was something in Row A and that's what this shows, but we still don't know where those somethings are. Now we look at the columns and create a new grid. If we do the same smearing of the information up the columns: remember Column 1 is 1, Column 2 is 0 Column 3 is 1 and Column 4 is 0, we get the grid of Figure 72(a).

We know there is something in Columns 1 and 3, but not where in that column they are. To finally solve the problem and recover the location of the ships, we just add these two grids with the smeared information together to get the grid of Figure 72(b).

In the combined grid, for example, A1 = 2+1 = 3, A2 = 2+0 = 2, A3 = 2 + 1 = 3, and so on. If we now look at this added together grid with the two sets of smeared data there are two peaks, of value 3, in positions A1 and A3. The peaks give the locations of the ships. We have an automatic ship finder but more importantly we have a way of recovering the actual position of the ships in the grid. We can

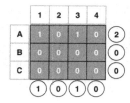

Figure 73: The reconstructed pond.

reconstruct the pond just from the clues: see Figure 73. We get it by using a set of results produced by adding together all the information along a row or a column. Now its time to weigh anchor and get back to the X-rays. As you probably guessed, that is what we were really working on all along.

Back to X-rays

An X-ray marks the spot

As an X-ray passes straight through your body, it is absorbed by all the bits of bone in the way. So, in effect, at a particular point on the X-ray plate, you have something similar to adding together all the 'ships' (bits of bone) along the X-ray's journey (say a row of the game board). So our X-ray is in fact like the set of numbers Row A = 2, Row B = 0 and Row C = 0. We know that the ray arriving at position A has gone through more bone (ships) than the rays going along Rows B or C. But we want to know how these bits of bones are related to one another. Are they close together or are they far apart. Both would give the same amount of absorption. So like our ship finder above we can rotate the X-ray source around the patient, so that it's coming in from the top rather than the side, and take another X-ray. This time our X-ray plate will show information of the form Column 1 = 1, Column 2 = 0, Column 3 = 1 and Column 4 = 0.

We can then take these two X-rays, do the smearing process (which is called *back projection* as you are smearing the data back to where it came from), and add the two back projected images together. In the same way, as the ship detector was able to find where the ships were in the grid, this mathematics tells you where the bits of bone were located in the body. And you don't need to just do two scans, you can rotate the X-ray source around the body taking thin scans at lots of different angles, then back project and add, so building a high quality image of a thin slice through the body.

The Beatles CAT

This method is called *CAT: Computer Assisted Tomography*. The first commercially viable CAT technology, was the EMI Scanner. It was developed by the record company, Thorn EMI, back in the 1960s. The story goes that they were able to fund this expensive medical research because of the money they made from The Beatles, arguably the most successful and influential pop/rock group ever. They needed to find some way to spend the enormous amount of money they were making! The mathematics for back projection had been around for a long time. However, until the medical applications and, more importantly, computers came along that could calculate the maths in a reasonable time, it had lain ignored, its revolutionary use undiscovered.

The inventor of the EMI Scanner, electrical engineer *Sir Godfrey Hounsfield*, was jointly awarded the Nobel Prize for Medicine, and later knighted for his efforts. Tomography is now used routinely in medicine, but is also used in archaeology to see inside Egyptian mummies, and in geophysics where you want to take slices through the earth. It's another example of how mathematics, computer science and engineering can all come together at the right time to completely change the way we do things.

Magnets and models

While X-ray tomography allows medics to see 3D pictures of the hard, X-ray absorbing bits in the body-like bones, it doesn't allow them to see the soft tissue in any detail. Unfortunately, its often in these tissues that disease can be lurking. Instead of X-rays, you need magnets. Enter, the field of *Magnetic Resonance Imaging* (MRI) and

MRI scanners. They can create 3D images of soft tissue in bodies, though need lots of computing to work.

MRI uses the properties of magnetism to build a body image. Water is made up of Oxygen and Hydrogen molecules, the latter having single protons at their core. The humble proton in water has a useful talent. It acts as a mini magnet, and its orientation, north–south pole wise, depends on what's happening to the protons in the water around it. Fortunately for us, human soft tissue contains lots of water along with other chemicals. That's what makes it soft.

To image inside the body, first a large, and uniform, magnetic field is applied inside the scanner where the person is lying. This field aligns all the protons in a slice in the person's body in the same direction. Next, to get an idea of position, a magnetic field is applied that varies from one side of the patient to the other. Its magnetic strength adds to the original unchanging field. This means that each position across the body has a different local magnetic field. If you hit the protons with the right radio frequency, they will absorb it then transmit it back. The frequency that the protons there will react to is determined by how strong the local field is. That depends on the density of protons and so how much soft tissue there is.

This reaction of the protons absorbing and transmitting a frequency is called *resonance*. Resonance happens in lots of different natural phenomena. A classic example is that wine glasses filled with different amounts of liquid vibrate at different frequencies to give different tones; they resonate at a frequency depending on the amount of liquid in the glass.

A slice of magnetism

The MRI system fires a pre-determined sequence of selected radio frequencies into the slice of the patient's body being scanned. It then measures the amount of signal that is resonated back for each. As each frequency transmitted in is tuned to one of the local frequencies across the slice, the outcome is a map showing the density of protons in particular locations, a map of the soft tissue.

You can get clever and from this basic system, using different imaging sequences of radio frequency pulses and gradients, calculate not just the amount of soft tissue but also its type, and something about the chemical environment it's sitting in, thus producing complex scans of useful medical data.

From these data sets it is possible, for example, to then produce a 3D-printed plastic model of someone's heart. The surgeon can actually hold a copy of the person's heart they will operate on to better understand the complexity of the operation they are about to do!

See it all in action

One of the more interesting applications of MRI is in being able to create movies of dynamic events in the body. Though the amount of computing power to create these currently means it takes a while to process them, they still remain useful. It's possible, for example, to create a movie of a beating heart inside the body, letting clinicians examine how valves open and close.

More exciting still is *functional imaging*, where by looking at the difference on scans of the places and rates that oxygen are used, its possible to uncover the activity in a live human brain as it thinks.

Oxygen rich and oxygen poor blood have different magnetic properties. When parts of the brain are used the amount of oxygen increases, so we can see which brain regions become active in any task we wish to give. We just need a control task, a task where that part of the thinking apparatus is not needed, and a task where it is. If we subtract the two digital images from each other, the areas left are areas when oxygen was used in the task, and from this we can start to explore how brains do what they do.

What is it that makes all these variations of 3D-imaging of the body possible. Ultimately it is based on underlying science and maths, but it is algorithms and so computational thinking that turns the recorded data into useful images.

More Measurement

Hot and happy

There are other ways to measure things inside us using computer technology. The human body likes to work at the correct temperature. It's the temperature where the various chemical reactions and body proteins' shapes work optimally, and we need them working well for good health. Being able to easily detect changes in temperature, pulse rate and other important values like the amount of oxygen in the blood is important. For example, if your blood isn't saturated you could die in less than 15 minutes. Unfortunately, the tests used to be slow and in the latter case, to determine the oxygen blood saturation, it even required samples of blood to be taken and tested in a lab. Not good if you only have 15 minutes to live. Today finding these values is the work of seconds, thanks to the combination of electronic engineering and algorithmic thinking as we will see.

A cave on the side of your head

Body temperature is measured by the temperature of the inside ear, a useful little cave on the head to the eardrum which provides a good measure of body heat. It's also a cave into which a small probe can be placed. A pyroelectric crystal in the measurement device is exposed to the infra-red radiation (that is just a long winded way of saying, 'heat') from the eardrum. It generates a charge in relation to the infra-red and the rest of the sensor technology uses algorithms that convert this charge into a digital measure of temperature.

Breathe deeply

Similarly, pulse and blood oxygen content can be measured using a sensor placed on the end of a finger. Infra-red light in the fingertip device is shone through the finger and how much of it is absorbed by the blood is measured. Your blood contains a protein called haemoglobin which make blood red, but more importantly carries oxygen around your body. Haemoglobin molecules with oxygen attached absorb the infra-red differently to 'unsaturated' haemoglobin with no oxygen. The trick though is to also include another light source sending out just red light. Red light more easily passes through blood that is full of oxygen, but is absorbed by it if there is no oxygen, the opposite happens to infra-red light. Used together, an accurate measurement of the amount of oxygen can be calculated. These two wavelengths: red at 660 nm, and infra-red at 940 nm, cycle through an on-off sequence. The data collected is converted, via a digital look-up table in the device (a handy **representation** that makes the job quick and easy), into a value for the oxygen level in the blood. The use of these pulsing sensors also allows the blood pulse to be estimated and so displayed on the device, too. Invented in the 1970s and first marketed in the 1980s the market for these sensors is now worth hundreds of millions of dollars.

Technology needs teamwork

Staying in hospital immerses you in high-tech computational thinking that can lead to improved healthcare. Medical information databases record your treatment, scan results and discharge letters. Micro-controlled wearable bumps use a carefully controlled vacuum to help heal wounds from the bottom up. Implanted smart pacemakers transmit daily heart beat data back to the hospital, and monitor for strange heartbeat behaviour, activated to prevent serious heart episodes. All this technology, and more involves programs doing the work. It all took a whole host of computational thinking to create. Algorithms alone aren't enough. Electronic engineers needed to build the sensors and other gadgetry. Before that though biochemists and physicists needed to work out the properties of the body and of fundamental things like protons, X-rays and magnetic fields. Mathematicians were also needed, devising the mathematics the algorithms are founded on.

There is one other massively important aspect to this use of technology. It all has to be easy to use for the doctors and nurses. It is there as a tool for them to use, and it can both save and take lives. Hospitals are busy stressful places and the technology needs to be built to take that into account. That means experts in psychology and human factors are needed too, to create usable technology.

To really make a difference, computational thinkers need to work in teams. They need to build on, and with, the work of people from many other specialities, if they are to do something really special and save lives.

Chapter 12

Computers vs Your Brain

Computers follow their programs precisely, doing exactly what the instructions tell them to do. Does our brain work like a computer? Are we logical? Can we follow our plans as accurately as a computer does? It turns out that our brains have some serious limitations and it leads to some pretty strange things. Understanding the weirdness helps us build better technology. One thing is clear though. Your brain is in control, not you.

Thinking Like a Computer?

Humans as computers

There are a lot of similarities between the human brain and a computer. Our ability to think, our intelligence, and sense of ourselves arises out of our brain doing lots of computation. The human brain, through its complex network of *neurons*, processes the information from the senses, decides what to do with it and turns this into our actions in the world around us.

Scientists don't yet fully understand how our brains work, but it's not surprising that it's still a challenge to comprehend. After all, it has been estimated the human brain contains as many neurons as there are drops of rain water in an Olympic size swimming pool. That is quite a lot!

A question we can ask is: do human beings think like a computer to help with everyday life? Does the way we think work as well as the way computers compute? If we are to do **computational modelling** of life, perhaps to build robots as successful as surviving as we have been, we need to first understand more about how we sense and understand the world. A related question we will start with though, is do we do computational thinking naturally?

Every day computational thinking

We've seen that our brains naturally do **pattern matching** applying something akin to production rules, just as computers are often programmed to do. We often respond to stimuli automatically, just following our in-built rules. For example, if the phone rings, I will pick it up without much thought. If there is a knock at the door, then I'm going to answer it.

Similarly, when we look at the way that we humans plan tasks, we find we employ computational thinking processes to let us do what we need to do. Take **abstraction**. We often use the idea of ignoring detail to simplify things we are doing: every time we take a complex situation we have to deal with and pull out only those parts that we think matter. Imagine describing your favourite TV show to a close friend. What you pull out would be different from the elements you might stress if you had to write an essay about it.

We use **decomposition**, setting goals and sub-goals when we plan. Going to the shops to buy the weekly shop could be our goal, and our sub goals could include remembering to take a bag, getting there, getting all the items, paying, and so on. That goal of 'getting all the items' breaks down again. While we are getting there we probably aren't thinking about the details of where the items are in the shop. While looking for eggs, we don't worry about where the breakfast cereal is. We package the problem into separate parts.

So we not only do computational thinking when trained to do it. We think like that fairly naturally, at least in some ways. Computer science training is about doing these things rigorously and in the context of precise algorithmic solutions.

Computer computational thinking

We've seen we are increasingly writing programs to allow the machines to do computational thinking too, not just computation.

Computer programs work using decomposition too. To make programs easier to write, programmers decompose instructions into separate steps, or procedures, just like we break our goals into subgoals. That means that, when executed, the program moves through the different stages of its plan to achieve the desired outcome in a similar way to us. They use **pattern matching** against *production rules* and machine learning systems allow them to see ever more complicated patterns. Vision programs use *filters* to hide detail, doing a form of **abstraction**. The more we chase *artificial intelligence*, the more we copy the skills of our brains. We've also seen, at the *neuron* level at least, thinking boils down to computation. So do we actually think like computers?

The differences between our brains and computers can start to show when we look more closely at the way we execute our plans. Just because we naturally do computational thinking doesn't mean we compute like a computer. Are we naturally able to follow the plans we make as perfectly as a computer does? No.

Puzzled planning

Here is a variation on an old puzzle for you to try. It will help us think about the way humans both plan and carry out their informal plans.

> A farmer is on her way to the local village with her sheepdog, Mist, who goes with her everywhere. To get to the village she has to cross a fast flowing river. An inventor living on the village side of the river has created a contraption to make it easier to get across. It consists of a rope and pulleys, with a seat hanging from the rope just big enough for one person. The locals have agreed to always leave the seat at the village side where the inventor lives so that it is easy for her to pack it away each evening: after all she is not charging anyone to use it. When she gets to the river, the farmer pulls the seat across from the far side using the rope. She gets in, hugging Mist, then pulls herself across and continues into the village.
>
> On one particular day she buys a new hen and a sack of corn. Returning home later in the day she arrives back at the ravine, and quickly realises she has a problem. She can only carry one thing across with her as she crosses using the seat. She will have to make

several trips. The trouble is, if she leaves the hen and the corn alone on either side, the hen will eat the corn. Similarly if she leaves Mist and the hen together on one side the dog will worry the hen and that may mean it stops laying eggs. Mist doesn't eat corn so it will come to no harm if left with him.

Write down the series of steps (an algorithm of course!) that the farmer must take to get everything across uneaten and continue on her way. Remember that the dog and hen must be kept apart as must the hen and corn.

Solve the puzzle before you read on.

Machine-making mistakes

We human beings split tasks we have to do into sub-goals, but it turns out that, unlike a computer, we tend not to tidy up the sub-goals as we finish them. It is all the result of our having limited *short-term memory*. If we have too much to remember right now, some things we know we have to do get dropped in favour of remembering more important things. What counts as most important to your brain? The goals you are trying to achieve, as opposed to other extra tidy-up tasks, are the things it gives priority to. It is easy to remember to turn on a light: you need to switch it on to be able to see what you are doing, but turning it off as you leave is easily forgotten. Why? Because you've achieved your goal in the room, and your brain has already moved on to the next big goal: the one that is taking you back out of the room.

How does this all apply to our puzzle? Well, many people solve the puzzle getting the farmer, dog, hen and corn safely across, but miss the last step. They don't send the seat back to the other end. We give one correct solution in Figure 74.

If you did forget to put that last step in your plan, you built what's called a *post-completion error* into your algorithm. You focussed on the goal, but forgot the sub-goal needed to do the clean-up. Here you made it at the planning stage. It is even easier to forget when just doing everyday tasks. People don't make this kind of error every time the possibility arises. It depends on how much else they are having to think about at the time. If your short-term memory is

1. Farmer travels across with the Hen (Dog left with Corn but that is okay).

2. Farmer returns.

3. Farmer travels across with Dog.

4. Farmer returns with Hen (as otherwise Dog will eat it).

5. Farmer travels across with Corn.

6. Farmer returns (leaving Dog and Corn again).

7. Farmer travels across with the Hen.

8. *Farmer sends the seat back to the other bank.*

Figure 74: A solution to the farmer's problem.

full of other things you need to remember, then you are more likely to forget these final tidy-up tasks. Different people have different amounts of this short-term, *working memory*, so some people will make this kind of mistake more often, but with enough other things to think of everyone makes them some times.

In this way, at least, therefore, we aren't like computers. They follow their plans exactly. Our brains struggle to, without help.

A helping machine hand

So we make mistakes, but machines can help us not to. Hole-in-the-wall cash machines are a good example of how the way a computer has been programmed can increase or decrease the likelihood of our making this kind of error. When cash machines were first introduced, you got the money, then you got your card back (it is still done like this in some countries). It turned out that lots of people walked off with their money, but without their card. Why? Because their goal was to get money. Once the main goal was achieved (they came for money and they had money) they left: moving on mentally to their next goal. The earlier sub-goal that they had completed, inserting the card, was forgotten... along with the fact that it left a new sub-goal to do later in retrieving the card.

The solution to this particular post-completion error is simple. The programmer must write the cash machine program, so that it doesn't release the cash (your goal) until you have taken the card (the tidy-up sub-goal). The design then forces you to tidy the sub-goal, before you achieve your goal. That is the way UK cash machines now work. It is not even the only solution. For example, at petrol stations, you might swipe your card, so you never give it up in the first place. Good design can help us overcome the flaws in the way our brains process information, but without the help, we make mistakes. Those designing and programming machines have to help. Sadly the lesson wasn't learnt more generally! When shops started to introduce self-service checkouts, some suddenly found that lots of people were forgetting their cards, having paid for their shopping. The **generalised** solution was ignored.

Losing your card, having to cancel it and get a new one is an inconvenience, but similar design flaws can be programmed into all sorts of devices. As we've seen, hospitals are full of computer wizardry that helps save lives, but if it is badly designed it can take lives too. Nurses need to set up infusion pumps to deliver drugs, for example. Exactly the same kind of design flaw as in the cash machines can exist in these devices. In setting up the machines, nurses need to close clamps to stop the flow of drug until everything is set. Once the computer pump is set up to deliver the right dose, they must be released again. That is exactly the kind of step that is easily forgotten, and nurses have much more on their minds, much more to deal with, than you do at a cash machine. This is exactly the kind of situation where the machine has to help not hinder.

Good computational thinking means designing computers to help overcome the 'flaws' that prevent our thinking like a computer.

Playing with Discrepancy: The Impossible Heist

Losing track

Our brains have to deal with a variety of limitations in the way they work, not just our limited amount of short-term memory. They also don't have perfect knowledge of situations, and they have to process vast amounts of information their senses are delivering to them quickly enough to react to the world around. It turns out that to do that, our brains make a wide variety of mistakes.

As we saw with cash machines, if we understand the sorts of mistakes that humans make, then we can design the systems (whether computer-based or otherwise) to prevent them. Sometimes, of course, we want people to make mistakes, to make assumptions that aren't valid. That is what magic is all about. So let's use a magic trick to explore a little more about how our brains struggle to see reality as it is, and get things wrong in ways that a computer-like brain would have no problem with.

We know that counting five coins left-to-right is exactly the same as counting them right-to-left. However, if we design a system that deliberately introduces a discrepancy, where two things that should be the same aren't, and the spectator doesn't notice, we can create a rather interesting magic trick from forcing the human error.

The impossible heist trick

Here is a classic movie plot-line you can perform for a friend. It has, like all good heist movies, a twist at the end. The cast of characters and props consists of two thieves and five gems. They are each played by an identical small coin: seven in total. Two coins represent the thieves and the remaining five represent the gems.

FADE IN: The story opens with the five gems laid out in a straight line on the table.

SCENE 1: The two thieves, represented by one coin in each hand make their play, as is traditional in heist movies, by descending from the ceiling on wires. You mimic this, starting from a position with both hands above the table showing their single coins, then close your fists and drop both hands down. The thieves now start to collect the gems; each hand moves in turn to take a gem (coin) from the table and put it into the fists until all the gems are removed.

SCENE 2: Dramatic moment: the final gem removed must have slipped, as the alarm goes off. The security guard will be on their way, so the two thieves quickly replace the gems, one by one, on to the table, and then zip upwards on their wires to a safe height to escape detection. The ruse works. The security guards see all five gems in place, reset the alarm, don't bother to look up and leave.

SCENE 3: The two thieves descend and again, collect the gems one by one from the table into their felonious fists. It looks like they will get away with it. But, in the final twist a security guard spots the two as they are about to escape over the roof and a fight entails represented by shaking the two fists in place above the table. Fight over, the two thieves are shown bafflingly caught together in one fist as it dramatically opens, and all the five gems have inexplicably gathered together in the remaining fist.

FADE TO BLACK: A mysterious and unexpected twist ending for an impossible heist, but how is it possible?

Let's go behind the scenes and look at the special effect, computational thinking and human biases that make it work.

What's happening behind the scenes?

This classic coin magic trick contains a clever algorithm, partnered with a beautiful manipulation of the viewers' brain, to bring about the seemingly impossible ending. The flow of the trick is exactly as given above, step by step, but there is one important detail missing. The trick uses a discrepancy, where your audience think the coins are in one state, while the reality is another. This discrepancy is related to how you pick up the coins or replace them on the table. Whenever you pick up coins from the table you start from the right of the row, so the right hand picks up the rightmost coin, then the left hand picks up the leftmost coin, then the right hand again picks up the rightmost remaining one, and so on. Now there are an odd number of coins. So, after the first right–left pick up sequence, there are four coins in your right fist, (a thief and three gems) and three coins in your left hand (a thief and two gems).

But when Scene 2 plays out, you put the gems back starting from the left, with the left hand, so that once the five gems are on the table again your fists actually contain two coins in the right hand and none in the left. However, that's where the discrepancy works. Your audience believe that we are back at the start with all gems on the table, and single thieves hiding in each fist. Now it's your job to convince them of that fake reality, without of course opening you fists. So you just tell them a tale, saying both thieves are back where they were, and shoot up their zip wires to hide.

Scene 3 is again a gem pick up from the table, so it starts at the right with the right hand, and after the familiar right–left sequence of pick-ups the trick is done for you as your right hand contains five coins and your left two coins, which you finally reveal as the two caught thieves and the five recovered gems.

Hiding the heist algorithm and state space

The pick-up right-to-left, replace left-to-right, pick-up right-to-left sequence is an algorithm, and this algorithm assures that each state your fists are in (the information about how many coins are in each fist) is exactly what's needed for the trick to work. Computationally, the result of applying left–right and right–left coin manipulations are not the same.

However, the viewers' inability to notice this discrepancy, reinforced by the story you tell, makes it hard for them to follow the real sequence of states. The trick is further strengthened by our tendency to remember information in a way that confirms our preconceptions (as set up here by the magician). This is known as *confirmation bias*. Looking back and recalling the effect, your audience will remember you were simply picking up and putting down coins, two actions which leave you where you started. This preconception is based on real world experience that, for example, laying forks on a table, then picking them up and putting them back again makes absolutely no numerical difference. That's absolutely right: most of the time it won't make any difference. However, with clever algorithmic manipulation of the underlying changes to the state, it leads to magic.

So we have found another way our brains get things wrong. We try to keep track of what is happening in the world, by making guesses, rather than tracking things exactly. Our guesses tend to confirm things we believe should be true, rather than necessarily things that are true.

Magical past to inspire your magic future

This heist version of the trick was developed specifically for this book, but of course you can come up with other ways to hide the algorithm by telling a story that suits your style. The basic trick has a long history, but it's mostly performed today using coins and the theme of thieves and sheep. The performers hands represent two barns, with a thief in each. Following the magical mechanics the five sheep coins are picked up alternately with both hands. At the end, both thieves magically end up in one 'barn', and all the 'sheep' in the other. In the past, this trick has also been performed with a whole variety of themes, including 'Sheep and Wolves', 'Cops and Robbers', 'Fox and Geese' and 'Poachers and Rabbits'. Paper pellets, matches and other small objects have been used. Many different magicians have created their own version of the trick. If you are interested, you can find out more by reading J. B. Bobo's, "Modern Coin Magic", which will also show you some useful magic sleight of hand techniques and other tricks to impress your friends.

The World of Illusions

Do our senses measure up?

Computers receive data from sensors, be it a light detection cell, a button press, GPS position or accelerometer. These data feeds are direct measures of the physical world. They are electrical signals in volts or amps, and by calibration of the sensors we know exactly what the measurements mean.

Humans have five rather fine senses: sight, taste, touch, smell and sound, but do they act like the sensors on a computer device? Or are they more complex and if so why? To explore this question, we need to enter the world of illusions. You are no doubt familiar with optical illusions, those fascinating pictures where the straight line looks curved, two similar objects look like they are different sizes, and so on.

From these illusions, we know that the eyes don't act like a simple camera sensor on a smartphone. They process the information before we use it and in some cases they produce mis-measures of the physical world. But what about our other senses? Here are some easy-to-do illusions that use things you can find around your home. You might be surprised by the results.

The sweetness illusion

The way we perceive taste can depend on more than what is being tasted. In particular, the *sweetness* of sugar depends on its *temperature*. So try this. Take sugar and water and mix them in a bowl. Then pour half the liquid into one glass and pop this glass in the fridge to cool. Take the remainder, pour it into another glass and leave it near a radiator to warm up. The science says that the perceived sweetness of sucrose (sugar) increases by 40 per cent as the temperature increases from 4°C (about fridge temperature) to 36°C (about body temperature). Take the two glasses of liquid and ask a friend which tastes sweeter (of course they both have the exactly the same proportion of sugar in them). If your friend says the warm glass is sweeter, then you have the *sweetness illusion.*

If you want to be really scientific about it, make more liquid in the bowl and put it equally into four glasses. Put one in the fridge, one by the radiator and leave the other two in the room. The two in the room are called the *experimental controls.* Ask your friend first to taste the sweetness of the two room temperature glasses. Because they have the same amount of sugar and the same temperature they should taste the same sweetness. That means our control will show that it is, in fact, the temperature that's causing the effect and not, for example, that the first glass drunk always tastes sweeter.

For even better science, it's also a good idea to have your friend swoosh their mouth out with normal water between tastes of the sugary water so you don't contaminate your samples.

The temperature illusion

Now try the *temperature illusion*. Take three glasses of water, put one in the fridge, fill the other with warm water from the hot tap (just warm NOT hot water) and fill the third with normal cold tap water.

Put the three glasses in a row in the order: warm, normal and cold. Pop a finger into the warm water and, with your other hand, pop a finger in the fridge-cold water. Leave for a short time, and then put both fingers into the middle glass. You will feel that the finger that was in the warm water feels cold and the finger originally in the fridge-cold water now feels warm, even though they are both now in the same temperature water.

What's happened here is that when your finger was, say, in the warm water it adapted to that temperature. Your body is really only interested in things that change in the environment, as it is the changes that you need to be able to react to. So, after your finger has adapted to the warm water, when it goes into the middle glass it is 'expecting' it to be warm. When it's not, your brain reasons, "this isn't warm so it must be cold". Similarly, the finger in the fridge water adapts to coldness, and when it moves into the centre glass, "that's not cold, so it must be hot". So one finger is saying hot, the other is saying cold, and both are actually at the same temperature.

The touch illusion

If you raid a DIY toolbox you can try a similar illusion: the *sandpaper touch illusion*. Carefully rub one hand on fine sandpaper, and the other on coarse sandpaper. Now rub both your hands on some medium sandpaper. It feels different to each hand. Why? Because the hand rubbing the fine sandpaper first adapts to feeling a fine roughness, whereas the hand on the course sandpaper adapts to lots of harsh roughness. So like the temperature illusion when your two hands have had their touch sensors adapted to different roughness, the medium paper will feel different to each. Predict, from the temperature illusion explanation, which hand will feel the medium paper as more rough, then try the experiment and see if you are right.

The size–weight illusion

This illusion, first described over 100 years ago, shows that if you lift two objects of equal weight, you will tend to perceive the smaller object as heavier. Take two empty plastic bottles of different sizes and, using scales, fill each with water or sand so they both weigh the same. Ask a friend to lift them up and ask which they think is heavier. If they say the smaller bottle, then the *size–weight illusion* is at work. You can even tell them the objects are the same weight. The illusion will still persist.

But things get even stranger! Researchers have found that when people alternately lift objects of the same weight but different size they apply the same fingertip force to both objects even though they still experience the size–weight illusion. One part of their brain is being fooled, telling you they are different, but another part of their brain isn't. It knows they are the same, but the two parts aren't communicating with each other!

Now you see it

Given our brains have lots of power to process incoming information from our senses, most of the time we are very aware of what's important and happening in the world around us. These experiments work because they are deliberately constructed to cause our brains to make a mistake, given the way they process that information.

However, what happens when that source of environmental information is poor or very messy? In that case, we can experience a special sort of illusionary phenomena called *pareidolia*. This happens when a vague and random stimulus (often an image or sound like a detuned television or radio) is perceived by us as significant. We see animals or faces in clouds, the face of the man in the moon, or claim we can hear non-existent hidden messages on vinyl records played in reverse.

Another thing you may not have considered is that your brain invents some of the things you 'see'. The *blind spot* in the retina of your eye is the place where the optic nerve leaves the eyeball, taking all those light signals to your brain. It has no light receptors on it at all, meaning that part of the retina can't physically see anything. So

Figure 75: The Blind Spot Illusion. Close your left eye and look at the +. Move the book backwards and forwards. The X disappears.

why is it that this empty, detector-less oval shape 1.5 mm in diameter isn't something you are aware of? Well, it turns out that your brain fills in the space. It actually makes information up to 'paper over' your blind spot. This so-called filling-in is quite sophisticated and depends on what's being observed in the real world around the blind spot. For example, close your left eye and focus with the right on the '+' in the image in Figure 75, then move the page backwards and forwards until the 'X' falls into your blind spot. Your brain will fill in the missing space with a continuous straight line.

So even when there is nothing there, your brain wants to find the familiar and expected patterns in the signals. If they are not there, it can make them up.

A Mathematical Model of the Mind

Weber's law

How does the physical world influence our senses? It's a profound question central to human experience that has troubled philosophers through the centuries. We sense the physical world around us, through, for example, measuring light intensity in the eye, detecting changes in air pressure in the ear, detecting changes in pressure on our skin, detecting chemicals in the air in our nose or chemicals in our food with our tongue; but how do these physical stimulation actually become a feeling of weight, or of hearing words, or of tasting delicious food? How does the measurement of the stimulus by the body become the experience of perception in the mind?

We still don't know the full answer, but back in 1860, a German doctor called *Ernst Heinrich Weber*, working with a colleague *Gustav Fechner*, discovered something rather fascinating. There is a simple mathematical rule (an equation rather than a *production rule*) relating the strength of stimulation to the strength of the perception, and it works across a whole range of our senses. This rule is called

Weber's Law, and it's one of the first examples of a mathematical model relating body to mind. While it was actually Fechner who did the maths, he gave the law as a 'gift' to Weber whose name it still carries.

A weighty psychophysics experiment

Weber carried out several classic experiments to help him devise the rule. He blindfolded a man and gave him a weight to hold. Slowly, Weber added more weight to the man's hand, until the man indicated he could first feel a difference. The weight was the stimulus strength, and the ability of the man to notice the difference in weight was the measure of a change in his perception.

What Weber found was that the amount of extra weight he could add until the man could just notice the difference depended on how much weight there was in the hand at the start. If the weight was say only 10 g to start with, adding 1 g more was noticeable. If the starting weight was say 1 Kg, then an extra 1 g added wasn't perceived. This type of experiment, where you manipulate something in the real physical world and measure the perception caused in a person's mind, is called *psychophysics*, and it was Weber and Fechner who started this whole field of research.

Say it with maths

In words, Weber's law says the stronger the original stimulus, the larger the change you need to make to notice that anything has changed. Words are always useful and Weber could describe his findings, but looking at the experimental data, Fechner was able to find a wonderfully simple mathematical description as well.

Let's call the stimulus strength, S. For example, here this would be the original weight in the hand. Suppose we can just notice the change if we increase the strength by amount dS (remember dS is the amount of extra weight we add when we notice it). The law says that if we divide the amount of extra weight by the original weight, we will always get the same number.

$$dS/S = k,$$

where k is a constant. It is a number you can work out from the experimental data.

I predict that...

If we measure the constant, k, for one particular weight (by taking the measurements and doing the division), we can then test if it is really the same for other weights. Better still, we can make predictions to test. Suppose we do it for a low initial weight of 10 g where we can just notice when 1 g extra is added. Weber's law says 1 g/10 g is a constant: here 0.1. Using this experimental constant, 0.1, we can predict how much we should be able to add to the hand (dS) if we started with 1 kg (1000 g). The law says $(dS/1000)$ must equal 0.1, so changing the subject of the formula

$$dS = 0.1 \times 1000 = 100\,\text{g}.$$

Our mathematics has made a specific mind-body prediction that we can now go and test. If we just used descriptive words, we couldn't achieve this useful testable ability.

Useful all round rule

Experimentally, psychophysics researchers have found that, if you don't go to extremes, then Weber's law is a good predictor relating stimulus strength to perception. The law holds for weight, the brightness of light, the loudness of sound and even the length of lines. It has many applications in computing such as in image displays, computer graphics and audio processing. For example, it can be used to decide what it is worth showing on a small screen. Why display detail that no one will notice because of the more obvious things around it? Similarly if you want to compress an audio file, so that it takes up less storage space, then algorithms based on Weber's Law can be used to decide what parts of the sound can be thrown away, never to be recovered, without anyone noticing: soft sounds near very loud ones, for example.

Weber's law is all around us, though you may not have noticed. Ask yourself this: why can't you see the stars in the daytime? They are shining just as brightly as at night. Why don't you notice the ticking of a clock in the noisy daytime, when it's there in the silence of the night? It's all just Weber's law hard at work helping us preprocess and cleverly compress that data going to our brains. Our brains do it so we can deal with a much larger range of inputs than we could just by measuring stimuli directly like a mechanical sensor.

Mimicking biology for better technology

Evolution has over eons found really clever solutions to hard engineering and information processing problems (but never filed a patent). There is now an active field of computer science research looking to understand how biological systems work called *Biomimetics*. An aim, once the biology is understood, is to build that understanding into computer systems. That way we get to test our understanding of the biology: does the computer system act with naturalistic properties. It means we can also make predictions. In addition, we get some very useful algorithms to help us build better computer programs. Science, computer science and computational thinking go hand in hand.

Computer scientists have found inspiration from nature to create a range of different algorithms that help us to carry out complicated tasks. The process of natural selection has developed clever engineering solutions to allow the creatures to survive on our planet. So why not copy them? After all, the wings of birds gave early aviators ideas for their aeroplanes. Why stop there. It's not just engineering problems that evolution has had to solve, it has also found ways to solve hard problems in information processing. Computer scientists have looked at how our *immune system* works, with its complex network of antibodies which allows us to fight disease. These antibodies work by matching the shapes on the antibodies to match the patterns of protein molecules on the surface of invading germs and others nasties. These networks can be mimicked on a computer so the algorithm carries a range of different digital patterns. This allows us to detect patterns in data, be it patterns in the word content of spam email or detecting suspicious traffic on a network.

Computer simulation of the ways that ants forage from their nests have also been used to help robots developed good solutions to improve their navigation. Measurement of *visual salience*, the property of areas of an image that draws our eye to it, have also been developed on computers based on an understanding of the way our visual cortex, the image processing part at the back of our brains, works. This allows robots to start to understand a scene and helps advertisers improve their graphic designs.

The continuous improvements in understanding biological systems will give computers new ways to work based on simplified versions of the workings of our natural world.

The Biased Brian

A street magic stunt: quick, think of a number

Street magicians often use this psychological trick. Ask a friend to quickly think of a two digit number between 1 and 100, both digits odd and both digits different from each other. Concentrate, the answer is... 37!

Magic: the statistical '37' number force trick

First up, this trick doesn't always work! Of course, in the TV shows they only show the times it did work! It's based on probability and a rather sneaky way of reducing your spectator's choice. If it goes wrong for you, then, hey, it's mind reading. It's supposed to be hard. You were just not tuned in properly.

How does it work?

You start by telling your volunteer that they can choose any 2-digit number between 1 and 100, and that means they will remember you giving them that 1–100 choice. It's called the *primacy effect* in memory: you tend to remember the things at the start better. Two digits means 1–9 are eliminated instantly.

You then go on to say both digits must be odd, so that halves the possible numbers too: all the even ones go. Next, you say both digits must be different. This narrows it down even more. There are in fact very few numbers left that the spectator can choose from (though they don't tend to notice this).

This is where the psychology and statistics comes in. When asked to give the number quickly, the vast majority of people will say 37. It may be that it's somewhere in the middle. 13 would be too small, 97 would be too big. It may be that the numbers 3 and 7, which themselves are the most common answers if you ask people to name a number between 1 and 10, just seem to come together. Whatever the reason, there is an increased chance that you get the 37 you want.

Psychology, bias and cognitive science

This effect of most people choosing 37 is called a *psychological bias*. Another example would be to ask someone to quickly think of a colour. Most people answer, RED. Or a vegetable? Most say, CARROT. Understanding human psychology, such as the primacy effect in memory and psychological biases used in this trick, is a part of *cognitive science*. It is a fascinating field where we try to understand the process of human thinking. Computer scientists then use the results to try, for example, to build easier to use software, or build artificial intelligences with human-like abilities. So the next time you think of 37, think of the cognitive science behind it, then choose the number 57 (or perhaps you did already!)

Bias, bias everywhere

If you toss a fair coin in the air 10 times, and each time it comes down tails, what's the chance of the next toss coming down head? Surely it must be more likely? Well of course not. Each toss is an independent 50:50 chance, each and every time. But most people feel strongly in this situation that heads just needs to turn up, even though there is no rational probability-based argument for it. It's a brain bias, called the *gamblers fallacy*. It is based on our tendency to think that future probabilities are altered by past events, when in reality they are unchanged.

It turns out that when we look in detail at the ways humans act themselves, or interact with one another in groups, we often don't make rational decisions. We don't follow, the logical and mathematical rules of a computer. We have seen how individuals make cognitive errors. They make mind slips like the one powering the coin trick, and we have already seen the example of a bias in the 37 trick. We also know our senses exploit Weber's law to help us usefully compress the data we get from our senses.

When we network lots of people together, some very strange bias effects begin to show socially as we process the information around us. They are probably a left-over from our distant, hunter-gatherer, pack-mentality past, together with social signals for selecting a mate that allow us to form more cohesive, bonded groups. However, they often lead to problems. Let's do a quick tour.

For example, the *backfire effect*, happens when people react to evidence against their view by actually strengthening their beliefs! The *bandwagon effect*, is our tendency to act the way others around us do. Combine these with *confirmation bias* we saw earlier, and you can see we our brains often make it hard work to get to the truth.

But our brain has thought of that: we have a built-in bias blind spot. We have a tendency to see ourselves as less biased than others. We are able to spot more biases in others than in ourselves. Our learning skills aren't immune from our bias problems. Social psychologists, David Dunning and Justin Kruger, found unskilled individuals have a tendency to overestimate their ability, while experts underestimate theirs.

You can use biases to become more popular. The *halo effect* means we tend to see positive or negative personality traits spill over from one area of personality to another. This tends to be a strong effect in those who are attractive. We tend to see attractive people as having virtues they don't really have, just because they are pretty. Once we are in a group, our *in-group bias* keeps that group stable. It is the in-built tendency we all have to lavish preferential treatment to others we perceive to be members of our own groups. There are also reports of the *Google effect* (other search engines are available!), a modern tendency for us to forget information that we know we can easily find using an Internet search engine. Perhaps this is our brain evolving to link with the technology around us, and let the computers take some of the strain!

There are many other social, memory and cognitive biases that result from the way our brains work, and we have to deal with them all. Often they are running in our brains at a sub-conscious level, so we aren't explicitly aware of them. However, they have been shown to fundamentally affect our behaviour and the behaviour of society.

Imperfect computers

We don't act like a computer, doing everything perfectly. But it's important to realise that computers are not perfect either, just in different ways. They do what their programs tell them to do. If the programs have bugs, then they will do the wrong thing. Worse than that, even if the programs do exactly what the programmer intended, they still may do the wrong thing, if the programmer's idea of what they should do is faulty. As we've seen they can be designed in a way that means they are a mistake waiting to happen. It could be that in rare cases, ones that the programmer didn't think through properly, they are programmed to do the wrong thing. The way they are programmed could be the reason people using them make mistakes. It is not just that they must do what is intended, it is that what is intended must be the right thing too.

When people believe in the infallibility of programs, bad things can happen. A UK court case of 2015 is an extreme example that illustrates this. Two nurses were charged with manslaughter after a series of stroke patients died. When police checked the records, they found discrepancies between the notes of the nurses and the computer logs of the machines used to take blood tests. Clearly the only explanation was that the nurses must have fabricated the records, to hide mistakes that led to the deaths. However, eventually when the court asked a computer science expert to examine the computer evidence, it became clear that it was the computer records that were unreliable, for all sorts of reasons. The case against the nurses collapsed. Police, hospital administrators and prosecutors had all up to that point taken it for granted that the machines told the truth, and as a result two innocent women could have gone to jail. You do not have to intend to follow a career as a programmer to need to understand how computers work, and how they don't.

Programmers on the other hand need to understand people. It is only if they understand our limitations, our biases, the way our senses work, can they write programs that are fit for purpose, that help people rather than make life difficult (well some of the time anyway).

Rhyme-as-reason

Let's finish with one final bias we humans suffer from that is worth noting just because it's so strange: the *Eaton-Rosen phenomenon*. This bias, often also called the *rhyme-as-reason effect*, means we have a tendency to judge a statement as more accurate or truthful when it is rewritten to rhyme. It's a trick often used by advertisers. Quite why a rhyming statement is seen as more truthful is open to debate. We may just feel it's more beautiful and has a pleasing aesthetic.

Great thing our brain. It's rather quaint, but a natural computational and logical thinker, it clearly ain't (well some of the time anyway). We do not think like a computer, though in future computers will increasingly be designed to think like us, and perhaps copy some of our quirks. Only then will they be able to experience the world as well as we do.

Chapter 13

So What is Computational Thinking?

We've run through lots of examples of computational thinking in action. Hopefully you now have a general idea of what computational thinking is all about, and how the different elements, like abstraction and algorithmic thinking, come together to give you a powerful way to both solve problems and understand the world. In this final chapter, we will run through all those different components that we have seen contribute towards the thing we call computational thinking.

Computational Thinking

Computational thinking is a loose set of problem solving skills that mainly focus on the creation of algorithms. Algorithms are powerful things because once created, they can then be used to do things without thought. Computer Scientists are interested in algorithms because they are the basis of programs, but people have been devising algorithms for thousands of years, long before computers were invented. Computational thinking is an old skill, even if the name is recent.

Algorithmic thinking is at the heart of computational thinking, but it also involves a series of other techniques including abstraction, generalisation, decomposition and evaluation. At its core are ideas of logical thinking, pattern matching and choosing good representations of data for the problem at hand. It draws on scientific thinking and, through approaches like computational modelling, is changing the way science is done. It relies on a deep understanding of people, their strengths and their weaknesses, if it is to be done well. Above all it is a very creative activity.

Let's look at the components in turn, many of which form the basis of other subjects, other problem solving approaches too.

Algorithmic Thinking

Algorithmic thinking is about seeing the solutions to problems as algorithms. For example, the route we came up with to solve the Knight's Tour and Tour Guide puzzles were sequence of instructions that can be followed to visit every tourist attraction or square of the board and get back to the start. Our solution is a simple algorithm for doing a tour of the city or of the board. There are several different routes you could take — several different algorithms can be solutions to the same problem. We saw that magic tricks are algorithms that magicians follow to guarantee the magical effect. Algorithms allowed us to win at Noughts and Crosses and communicate clearly with people with locked-in syndrome. There are algorithms for learning and more generally they give us a way to create intelligent machines. Algorithms make money and art. They even save lives, for example when embedded in medical devices.

Why is it important to write down an algorithm when we solve a problem? Well, once we write the algorithm down we can follow it as many times as we want (give tours over and over again, always play a game perfectly, save the life every time...) with no more problem solving work, without having to work out how again and again. We can even give an algorithm to someone else to follow (your junior assistant if you are the Tour Company Manager, perhaps; anyone who visits the locked-in syndrome patient in hospital; your apprentice magician, ...). Then you won't need that person to have to work it all out for themselves from scratch. Algorithms are no longer things for humans to follow, as they were for thousands of years. In the age of the computer, they can also be turned into programs, and then machines can do the work instead.

Computational modelling

A massively important part of algorithmic thinking is the idea of **computational modelling**. This is the idea that you can take some thing in the real world, the weather say, that you want to understand better and create an algorithm that does the same thing in a virtual world. The algorithm simulates it. By running the algorithm, you can make predictions about what the real thing will do: predict whether it will rain tomorrow or not, for example. Once you have a good computational model you can run lots of experiments on the simulations. That can be done far faster than experiments in real life. You can even use maths to reason about the consequences of the model in general.

Computational modelling is the main way that computational thinking is transforming every other subject. We have seen computational models of how the brain works and how ecosystems function, for example. They are also used in biology where biologists create algorithmic models of things like the heart, or of cancer cells, so that they can then do virtual experiments. They give a way to reduce the number of animals used in experiments too. Run the experiments on a virtual animal instead. In economics, computational models of the economy can be used to predict what the range of possible effects changes the politicians are planning might actually be. Climate scientists use models to predict the range of possible consequences of global warming. It is being used to understand creativity too, including what makes good literature or art.

Computational modelling is being used in physics, in biology, in chemistry, in geography, in archaeology... and lots of other subjects too. It gives a new way of doing your subject, whatever your subject actually is. All these things are also being turned by innovative people into new business niches, creating the industries of the future.

Computational modelling has even changed the way we play games. Games like World of Warcraft are just a computational model of a fantasy world; sports games are computational models of the sport. In both cases, a model of the laws of physics is built into the program, so that, for example, what goes up comes down again!

The rise of computational modelling is a key reason why whatever subject you do, having computational thinking skills, not just digital literacy, or IT skills, is massively important.

Scientific Thinking

Scientific thinking is also important for computational thinkers. To support the scientific process such as with computational modelling, you need to understand how good science works. For example, it is important to realise that results about a model are just that. They tell you things about the model. If the model doesn't match reality, then the results are nothing to do with reality. You need to check any results are valid in the real world by making new predictions and then testing them. However, if you don't lose sight of that point, computational thinking provides a powerful way to understand the world. Scientific thinking is needed in other ways to, and in particular as part of evaluating algorithmic solutions. Scientific methods provide a set of ways of checking algorithms are fit for purpose, a point we will return to below.

Heuristics

Sometimes it's not actually possible to create an algorithm that guarantees to get the best solution for a task, either at all or within the time available (and we really do mean impossible, not just hard). In those situations, a **heuristic** algorithm is used instead. Heuristics don't guarantee the best solution but just give a reasonable solution in a reasonable amount of time. Heuristic problem solving is needed to come up with algorithms like that. They don't always get the best answer but aim to usually get a good answer. That's essentially what your sat nav is doing whenever it plots routes for you.

Logical Thinking

Thinking algorithmically involves **logical thinking**: being very careful and precise about details. The instructions in an algorithm, for example, have to cover every eventuality. Did you think to include in your instructions for adding numbers what to do with negative numbers as well as positive numbers? If you didn't, then a computer might either give the wrong answer or crash when confronted with the problem. As you develop an algorithm, you need to think very logically about how it works. In your head at least, if not on paper, you have to have a logical argument of why it always works. You don't want your Mars lander to crash just as it is finally landing on Mars months after it set off, just because you forgot a detail. Logical thinking is a part of **evaluation** too as we will see.

Pattern Matching

Spotting when two problems are the same (or very similar) is an important part of computational thinking: **pattern matching**. It is something we do naturally all the time and is the way experts work, recognising a situation and without thinking just doing the right thing. It is at the core of the way many programs work too: they match rules against the situation to determine the appropriate set of instructions to follow. The programmers developing such programs have to work out the patterns the program will match against. Machine learning is all about matching patterns too, but now the programs themselves work out the patterns themselves.

In problem solving, pattern matching saves work, as it allows us to avoid going through all the same hard work every time we are given a new problem. Match a problem to one you've previously solved and just pull out the old solution. When you see a problem or puzzle about the way different places are linked, for example, think about graphs. Another way of saying that is if you can match a problem to the pattern of moving from point to point, then use a *graph* to represent it. The points don't have to be physical places. They could be web pages (with hyperlinks between them), alarm clock states (with button presses that move between them), cities (with flights between them), and so on.

Representation

We can make a problem easier to solve by choosing a good **representation** of it. It is just the way that we organise information. There are surprisingly many ways we can represent the same information, and once you realise that and focus on choosing a good representation at the outset, problems become easier. Good representations can make things much easier for humans as well as computers as we saw with our graph problems and with the game of Spit-not-so. However, they can also completely change the algorithm we use to solve a problem. Instead of a slow and complex algorithm, we might find we have unlocked the possibilities of a quick and simple one. We have seen different representations throughout the book, such as *raster* representations for images, storing lots of *pixels* that make up a grid vs storing *vectors*: lines and shapes. We've seen how grid representations unlock all sorts of possibilities. We've also seen that if numbers are stored as binary on punch cards, then fast search and sort algorithms are possible. Representing a pattern as a *digital filter* leads to algorithms that can help computers see. Choosing a good representation, it turns out, is also an important part of **abstraction** and **generalisation**.

Abstraction

Abstraction is the hiding of details in some way to make a problem easier to deal with. There are lots of different ways you can hide details. It can be done when designing algorithms and when **evaluating** them.

For example, one very important use of abstraction, we saw in some of our early magic tricks, and called **control abstraction**, is in grouping instructions together so that you have instructions that do bigger steps. The idea here is that you are hiding the details of the individual steps needed. Recipe books do this all the time. They say things like "boil the potatoes". That involves lots of steps: filling a pan with water, turning the heat on, bringing it to the boil, adding the potatoes, and so on. All those steps are brought together into a simple command "boil the potatoes". To follow the instructions you need all the detail, but it helps in writing down instructions and when thinking about the algorithm (or recipe) as a whole to work with the big steps. All that detail is too much to think about until you are actually doing it and need the steps. This form of abstraction is linked very closely to **decomposition** that we describe below.

Another kind of abstraction, called **data abstraction**, is where you hide the details of how data is stored: how it is really **represented**. For example, numbers are actually stored in a computer in binary: as a sequence of 0s and 1s. The number 16 might be stored actually as 00010000. We ignore that fact when thinking about numbers though. We just think of them as the decimal numbers like 16 that we know and are used to using. When we write programs we use decimal numbers in the instructions, not binary. Our programs ask the people using them to enter numbers in decimal instead of binary too. Ultimately though the computer works with binary numbers. No one using the program has to know that the numbers are actually stored like that: that detail is hidden.

We don't just use abstraction when writing programs. We can also use it when evaluating them. For example, as we saw, when exploring algorithms to help a person with locked-in syndrome, if we want to decide which of two different algorithms that do the same thing is the quickest, we don't need to think about time itself. We can hide the detail of actual time and think about work done instead: how many operations do you need to follow with each algorithm to get the job done. If one algorithm involves following 100 instructions, and the other only 10, then the second is going to be the quickest. We can work that out just by counting the operations, without timing anything at all. We hide the detail of how much time operations take to make the problem easier.

Generalisation

Generalisation is the idea of taking a problem we have solved and adapting the solution (the algorithm) so that it solves other similar problems. For example, suppose we have to find our name in a seating plan: it's just a list **representation** of names that tells us where to sit. Rather than looking randomly, we might start at the top of the list and check each name in turn until we come to ours. On another day, we have to find a CD on a shelf. We might recognise that it is the same problem. In doing so, we are **pattern matching**: matching one problem to another. Once we have realised two problems are the same in this way, we can use the same solution for both. We don't need to come up with an algorithm from scratch. We start at one end and run our finger along the shelf, checking each CD in turn until we find the one we want (or get to the end meaning it isn't there). We have generalised or transformed the algorithm (the solution to the first problem) so that it can be used to solve the new problem.

We can take this a step further if we realise that any time we have a sequence of things lined up in some way and have the problem of finding something in it we can use this solution. We have now generalised the problem of finding a name to finding anything, and generalised the list of names to any sequence of things lined up. We have transformed our algorithm into a general *search algorithm*. It is an algorithm that doesn't just solve one problem, but any problem of that kind. It can be used any time we are searching for something. We have generalised a solution that was invented to solve just one problem (finding our name) to be solutions to a whole class of problem.

Notice that to do the generalisation, we also needed to hide some of the detail. We don't want to think about the detail of names or CDs, so we generalise that into being 'a thing'. We are using **abstraction** to do the generalisation.

Sometimes, we do generalisation in this way to create very general algorithms that we can use in lots of situations as above. At other times, we just realise that a new problem in a completely new area is similar to something we have done before, so we do a one-off generalisation of it — transforming the problem (and so solution) from one domain to the other. For example, phones use predictive texting. As you type a word, the phone guesses from the letters typed so far what the whole word will be. People who are totally paralysed and cannot speak, communicate by spelling out words a letter at a time by blinking their eye. The same predictive texting algorithm can be used in this situation too. The people working out what is being said can guess the whole word early in the same way. The same algorithm can be used for two apparently different problems once you realise there are similarities by **pattern matching**.

Pattern matching and generalisation can be used at all sorts of levels, from spotting that a whole problem is the same as one we've solved before to realising that a small fragment is similar. Often as we build up a program, individual parts of it are similar to things we've come across before — perhaps we need the program to repeatedly ask if we want to do something again (like play the game again when we win). If we have written code for that before, then realising this is the same, we can just adapt and reuse that bit of code, integrating it into our new program, without having to think through the commands needed from scratch.

Generalisation can also be helpful for **evaluation**. Suppose we have created some general algorithm. We can evaluate it once and everything we learn about it applies to every new use of it. For example, once we know how fast our algorithm is, and how it compares to other algorithms that do the same thing, we can use that in deciding whether it is appropriate for some new job.

Decomposition

Decomposition involves breaking a big problem into smaller problems that are easier to solve. We can solve the big problem by solving each of the small problems individually. We saw this when building our scam bot, for example. We could build the whole by thinking separately about lots of individual components of it. This is a really powerful way to think about solving problems. It is decomposition that has allowed us to write complicated programs that are millions of instructions long. Without that, we would not have programs doing all the things computers are now used for.

Decomposition is used in writing programs in a way that links closely to **control abstraction**. The idea is to break a program you are writing into lots of separate tasks. You then write separate little programs for each of those smaller tasks. Each of those small programs is easy to write. The bigger program that combines them is easier to write too, as you don't have to think about all the details at once. Once the parts are complete, you only have to think about what they do, not how they do it. To make that easier, you give each a name that makes clear what it does but hides the detail of how it does it (and naming things like that is another kind of **abstraction**). Then when you put the small programs together to make the big one, you don't have to think about all the fiddly detail anymore.

Decomposition in this way gives another way of using **generalisation**. If the smaller programs are written in a suitably general way, then you may be able to use them again in other big programs. You may even be able to just take existing programs to solve some of the sub-problems if you can **pattern match** them to existing things.

There are some special techniques used to do decomposition in a way that makes it easier to come up with solutions that work really quickly. One is *divide and conquer problem solving*. The idea here is to solve a problem by finding a way to break it into smaller but otherwise identical problems. To solve the problem of searching through a telephone directory, we can open it in the middle and see if the names on that page are before or after the one we are looking for. We then know which half to search ignoring the other half. We now have a similar but smaller problem: searching half a telephone directory. We solve that in the same way, going to the middle of the remaining half and so on, till we find the name we are looking for. That gives a far faster solution. Thinking in this way is an example of *recursive problem solving*: a special form of **algorithmic thinking**. It is the basic idea of writing algorithms that break problems into similar smaller problems. The special thing about divide and conquer over recursion is the idea of splitting the problem into halves (or thirds, quarters, etc.) so that each new problem is roughly the same size and a lot smaller and so easier to solve than the original.

Understanding People

Technology is ultimately there to be used by people and to support people. That means computational thinking is really about problem solving for people, not about technology. Therefore, **algorithmic**

thinking has to include an element of **understanding people** and especially understanding their strengths and weaknesses. We've seen that over and over, from helping people with locked-in syndrome, to making sure nurses don't make mistakes. Here is another extreme example to make the point. Suppose you are designing a security algorithm to keep your online banking system secure. You might come up with an algorithm that requires people to enter a password that is 1000 letters long and must be made of random letters with no recognisable words within it. That would be really secure! It would also be very silly. Apart from an odd genius or two, no human could reliably remember a password like that. The algorithm would be useless. Understanding people has to be at the centre of computational thinking problem solving.

Evaluation

Once we have written down an algorithm, it is important that we evaluate it. We must check that it works. In particular that means that we must check that the algorithm meets a set of properties, or *requirements*, that describe the problem.

Evaluation is about checking that your solution is a good solution that is fit for purpose. There are several different kinds of things that you need to evaluate. The most basic is *functional correctness*: does your algorithm actually work? Always! Whatever happens will it always do the right thing and give the right answer? You need to be sure it does. Otherwise a person, or machine, trying to follow it later could be left high and dry, blindly doing the wrong thing, or not knowing what to do. We saw that, for example, in the magic trick guessing objects. We seemed to have covered every eventuality, but it could still go wrong if the person picked one of our secret objects. Neither magicians nor computers should be left in an unplanned for situation.

Another thing that you might evaluate is *performance* in the sense of speed. How fast is your algorithm? Are there other algorithms that would do the job more quickly? Are there particular situations where your algorithm is slow? Do those situations matter?

For example, one algorithm used to sort things into order (called *quicksort*) is generally really fast. However, if you give one version of it, a series of things to sort that just happen to be in the right order already, it is ridiculously slow. It takes longer to sort things that are already sorted than things that are completely mixed up. It is a great algorithm, but it would be silly to use if you knew you had a pile of things that were almost in the right order already. There's rarely a single best algorithm for a task. It depends on the situation, and you need to evaluate how well an algorithm fits that situation.

A third really important part of evaluation is about whether the solution you have come up with is actually fit for purpose. Algorithms are there to solve problems for people, as we have seen. They must work in a way that allows people to use them as we saw when talking about algorithmic design. You therefore have to evaluate programs, systems and solutions generally for how easy they are to use and how good an experience it is for people who are using them. You do not want them to lead to people making mistakes, and you don't want them to lead to people being frustrated or angry. That in particular involves understanding people. What you are really asking in this kind of evaluation is "Does it work well given the way people are? Does it play to our strengths and limit the problems caused by our weaknesses?"

Suppose you are designing a medical device to deliver a pain relief drug to patients. The nurse sets up the dose, hits go and it then pumps drug through a tube into their arm over several hours. Now obviously you want it to be functionally correct. If the prescription is to deliver 15.5 milligrams per hour for 6 hours, and that is what the nurse programs, then that is what it should do. It also has to work suitably quickly. It's no good if the nurse has to wait several minutes after typing in the dose before it will start because it is taking a long time to set itself up. Nor should it stop mid-infusion because it needs to do some slow tidying of its memory. Even more importantly it should be easy to use. It should help prevent the nurse making mistakes and help recover if a mistake is made. If the nurse enters 155 instead of 15.5 by mistake, and that is a dangerous amount of that drug, then the machine should at least warn the nurse, and give them a chance to undo their mistake. Better still it should be designed to make such mistakes less likely in the first place.

There are very many techniques, and so skills used in evaluation. It involves *rigorous testing*: being very, very organised about the way you check that an algorithm or program implementing it actually works. That involves doing lots of testing, not just trying the program once or twice and deciding it always works. It also involves being clever in the way you pick what situations to test to increase the chances that there are no surprises. That in itself takes some **logical thinking** about what you need to test to be sure you have good coverage of the possibilities.

A. complimentary approach to testing is *rigorous argument.* Rather than running a program to see if it works we can use the power of argument. Using *logical reasoning*, we can come up with an argument as to why certain tests are enough to guarantee the whole is right. Taking this to an extreme, our arguments can be about why the algorithm or program as a whole always works using logical proof, a variation on the kind of proofs that mathematicians do. When you create an algorithm or program, you have in your head reasons why you think it works. At the evaluation stage, you are checking those reasons, and making sure you haven't missed any detail. Often such proofs are done on an **abstraction** of the system. That just means irrelevant details are ignored to make the proof easier to complete. Its important, though to realise when your results apply to models of the system, and when to the system itself. Just because a model is right, doesn't always mean the system itself is.

You can also evaluate different parts of a solution separately. This is a use of **decomposition** where we think of a problem or a system as a lot of simpler parts that can be worked on separately. As those parts are smaller, that is simpler. Evaluation is not something you just do at the end when you have a solution, you do it as you come up with solutions, as you develop the algorithms, the programs and their interfaces. You have to do it repeatedly as you develop a solution, creating early prototypes and evaluating them in different ways, solving problems that arise. **Decomposition** helps as it allows you to evaluate each smaller part separately as you complete it. You can check each part is ok and fix any mistakes you do find before you worry about whether the whole thing works.

When it comes to evaluating whether our solutions are fit for purpose, we can also use methods a bit like testing where we try out the system: *observational methods*. The difference is that this kind of evaluation involves real people using the system we are evaluating. One way is to set up experiments where we watch people using our system in lab conditions: essentially running scientific experiments. Another is to go out 'into the wild' and watch the system being used for real. In both cases, we are looking for things going wrong, or things that people have difficulties with, asking ourselves all the time: "could we change the system to make things easier for people".

We can again use *analytical methods* and *logical reasoning*. This essentially involves getting experts who understand people, and also understand what makes good or bad design, to look at a system in a very organised way. Their aim is to predict potential problems: things about the system that people are likely to struggle with. They might, for example, step through a particular task, and ask at each step "How might a person misunderstand what to do here?" The experts might use specific principles as guidance like: "It should always be possible to undo the last step if a mistake is made." If they find a situation where undo isn't available, then that can be reported as a problem to fix.

Creativity

A further skill involved in *algorithmic design* is that of **creativity**. Algorithmic design is a very creative process. You can do it in a very plodding way, of course: turning the handle on some basic techniques, and that is the way most people start. Brilliant computer scientists, though, come up with completely new algorithms either for old problems or completely new ones. They see opportunities no one has thought of before. Coming up with the ideas of how to turn their concept into reality is also obviously creative. The other parts of computational thinking involve creativity too. **Abstraction** itself requires a certain amount of it in working out the best details to hide to make the job as easy as possible. Similarly, **generalisation** and **pattern matching** sometimes need big creative leaps to see the links between apparently different situations. Even **evaluation** needs creativity in coming up with logical arguments or ways to explore situations. How do you evaluate how easy it is to use a mobile app in the actual situations it will be used. In a lab, you can watch everything they do. In the wild thats not possible... or is it? One early and enterprising evaluator, faced with this problem, came up with an evaluation hat for subjects to wear containing cameras watching what they did as well as what was happening around them.

Creativity needs the right conditions. The people involved need a playful state of mind and situations that promote it. It helps to want to have fun, so it's lucky that computing is so much fun. You need to have the time and space to let your mind wander. You need to be free from too much stress, from deadlines that must be met. Of course, the most creative ideas don't come from individuals but from groups of people bouncing ideas about, feeding off each other's creativity. Companies (and countries) that can promote that sort of work place are really going to change the world! Its no surprise that some of the biggest, most successful computer-based companies do exactly that.

That's because it's not just coming up with the algorithm that takes creativity. Sometimes the creativity is also in coming up with the problem to solve. It is about coming up with a transformational idea: the idea that once we have the algorithms to do something new, it really does change the way the world works. Devising an algorithm unlike any that has been seen before is the way to completely transform a problem, and that can transform the way we live our lives. That's especially so if you are creative enough to see a problem to solve that no one else has even noticed before... and then solve it. Out of creativity comes **innovation**, and that needs people who actually have the drive and skill to push an idea through to the end. All those big computer-based innovations like the web, social networking, online shopping, and so on, needed people with lots of creativity to start with, and then a mix of people with different skills, like business skills, to make them a reality.

Summary

Computational thinking is made up of many different skills. It's important to realise that these areas are not really distinct activities. Computer scientists actually use them all together in a rich and linked way when solving problems using computational thinking. Many of the skills also overlap with skills used by mathematicians, design specialists, scientists, engineers, as well as writers, historians, and more. Computational thinking as practised by computer scientists is the skill set that you get when it is all pulled together in this rich way, and that gives a different way of thinking about both problems and systems. Ultimately, of course, computer scientists are using the skills as a basis of creating machine-based solutions. It is through turning algorithms into programs that this way of thinking has changed the way we all live, work and play and will continue to do so in the future.

Computational thinking is not the way computers think. It is the way humans need to think to make computers do amazing things, but as we develop more powerful artificial intelligences, then increasingly we are programming the machines to do computational thinking too.

01110100 01101000 01100001 01101110 01101011 01110011
00100000 01100110 01101111 01110010 00100000 01110010
01100101 01100001 01100100 01101001 01101110 01100111
00100000 01101111 01110101 01110010 00100000 01100010
01101111 01101111 01101011 00100000 00001101 00001010

Further Reading

We have been reading about maths, magic and computing for 40 or so years, so here are some of our writing and some of the writing that have inspired us along the way.

Is it computing?

Computing is everywhere once you start to look, and not just in machines.

Computer Science for Fun www.cs4fn.org
> Thousands of articles looking at every aspect of the fun side of computing as well as magazines and booklets.

Teaching London Computing
> www.TeachingLondonComputing.org
> Resources for teachers for teaching interdisciplinary computational thinking including support material for many of the topics in this book.

Computing Without Computers Paul Curzon, v0.15, Feb 2014.
> Available from teachinglondoncomputing.org/resources/ins piring-computing-stories/computingwithoutcomputers/.

Computational Thinking: HexaHexaflexagon Automata
> Paul Curzon, Queen Mary University of London, 2015
> Hexaflexagons turned into a way to explore finite state machines.

Algorithmic puzzles Anany Levitin and Maria Levitin, Oxford
University Press
More algorithmic puzzles than you thought existed, used to
help develop algorithm design strategies.

Nine algorithms that changed the future John MacCormick,
Princeton University Press, 2012
An in-depth look at the big algorithms that have changed the
way we live our lives.

Goedel, Escher and Bach Douglas R. Hofstadter, Basic Books,
1979
A Pulitzer prize winning tour de force in the spirit of Lewis
Carroll about mind, machines, computation, proof, patterns,
the power of rules and more.

CS Unplugged csunplugged.org/
Where unplugged computer science started. Includes a book
of classroom activities to download.

Is it maths?

Many books claiming to be recreational maths are really full of
computer science games, puzzles and curiosities. Here are some of
our favourites.

Mathematical puzzles and diversions Martin Gardner, Pelican, 1965
Hexaflexagons, how to win at noughts and crosses and Nim,
card tricks and much more.

More mathematical puzzles and diversions Martin Gardner,
Pelican, 1966
Mazes and mechanical puzzles.

Further mathematical diversions Martin Gardner, Pelican,
1977
Includes learning machines and solitaire.

Mathematical carnival Martin Gardner, Pelican, 1978
Includes lightning calculations and shuffles and Hot, the game Spit-Not-So is based on.

Mathematical circus Martin Gardner, Pelican, 1981
Includes whether machines can think, Boolean algebra Fibonacci sequences and optical illusions.

Winning ways for your mathematical plays Berlekamp, Conway and Guy, Academic Press, 1982
Analyses many different games and puzzles and has a major overview of Life from the people who invented it.

The magical maze Ian Stewart, Phoenix, 1998
Graph representations, exploring mazes, magic and more.

The Moscow puzzles Boris A. Kordemsky, Edited by Martin Gardner, Translated by Albert Parry, Penguin, 1975
Lots and lots of algorithmic and other puzzles.

Why do buses come in threes? Rob Eastaway and Jeremy Wyndham, Robson Books, 1998
Includes graphs, everyday logic and magic.

How long is a piece of string Rob Eastaway and Jeremy Wyndham, Robson Books, 2003
Fractals. packing problems and proof.

The Puzzler www.puzzler.com
We do all sorts of puzzles from all sorts of places, but the Puzzler is one wonderful source.

Is it magic?

There are very many books on magic. Here are a few that inspired us.

Self-Working Card Tricks Karl Fulves, Dover, 1976
A whole book full of algorithmic, self-working card tricks.

Modern Coin Magic J. B. Bobo, Dover 1982
Includes self-working tricks with coins.

Magical Mathematics Persi Diaconis and Ron Graham, Princeton University Press, 2013

Magic and Showmanship Henning Nelms, Dover, 1969
A more general book on the skills of a magician.

Is it something else?

The design of everyday things Donald E. Norman, MIT Press, 1998
Learn about design and usability from everyday things in a way that applies in the virtual world too.

Sources of Power Gary Klein, MIT Press, 1999
How experts do things, suggesting intuition is really pattern matching.

The Diving-Bell and the Butterfly Jean-Dominique Bauby, Harper Perennial, 2004
An amazing book about a love of life: living with locked-in syndrome.

Based on ...

The chapters of these books are extended reworkings of our writing for cs4fn, Teaching London Computing and other sources. The originals also include:

Computational thinking: searching to speak Paul Curzon, Queen Mary University of London, 2013
A shorter, earlier version of Chapter 2 on locked-in syndrome.

Cut Hive Puzzles Paul Curzon, Queen Mary University of London, 2015
A shorter, earlier version of Chapter 4 that introduced Cut Hive puzzles.

Computational thinking: Puzzling tours Paul Curzon, Queen Mary University of London, 2015
A shorter, earlier version of Chapter 5 on graphs.

Mini-megalomaniac AI is already all around us, but it won't get further without our help Peter W. McOwan. The Conversation. June 2, 2015. Available from: theconversation.com / mini-megalomaniac-ai-is-already-all-around-us-but-itwont-get-further-without-our-help-42672. A shorter version of the section on AIs ruling the world.

Index

Printed in the United States
By Bookmasters